D0000221

Chicken Soup
for the Soul.

Devotional Stories
for
Tough Times

Chicken Soup for the Soul: Devotional Stories for Tough Times
101 Daily Devotions to Inspire and Support You in Times of Need
Susan M. Heim and Karen C. Talcott. Foreword by Mary Beth Chapman

Published by Chicken Soup for the Soul Publishing, LLC   www.chickensoup.com

Copyright © 2011 by Chicken Soup for the Soul Publishing, LLC. All Rights Reserved.
No part of this publication may be reproduced, stored in a retrieval system or transmitted in any form or by any means, electronic, mechanical, photocopying, recording or otherwise, without the written permission of the publisher.

CSS, Chicken Soup for the Soul, and its Logo and Marks are trademarks of
Chicken Soup for the Soul Publishing LLC.

Scriptures taken from the Holy Bible, New International Version®, NIV®. Copyright © 1973, 1978, 1984, 2011 by Biblica, Inc.™ Used by permission of Zondervan. All rights reserved worldwide. www.zondervan.com.

The publisher gratefully acknowledges the many publishers and individuals who granted Chicken Soup for the Soul permission to reprint the cited material.

Front cover photo courtesy of iStockphoto.com/ diane39 (© Diane Diederich).
Back cover photo courtesy Camille Akers Blinn, camilleblinn.com, http://camilleblinn.com. Interior photos courtesy of Photos.com

Cover and Interior Design & Layout by Pneuma Books, LLC
For more info on Pneuma Books, visit www.pneumabooks.com

Distributed to the booktrade by Simon & Schuster. SAN: 200-2442

Publisher's Cataloging-in-Publication Data
(Prepared by The Donohue Group)

Chicken soup for the soul : devotional stories for tough times : 101 daily
   devotions to inspire and support you in times of need / [compiled by] Susan
   M. Heim [and] Karen C. Talcott ; foreword by Mary Beth Chapman.

   p. ; cm.

   Summary: A collection of 101 Christian daily devotional stories on times of trouble in people's lives, by various authors comprising a piece of scripture, a personal story illustrating the piece of scripture, and a relevant prayer.
   ISBN: 978-1-935096-74-0

   1. Christian life--Literary collections. 2. Christian life--Anecdotes. 3. Suffering--Religious aspects. 4. Consolation--Prayers and devotions. 5. Devotional literature. I. Heim, Susan M. II. Talcott, Karen C. III. Chapman, Mary Beth IV. Title: Devotional stories for tough times

PN6071.C56 C45 2011
810.8/02/0382/48   2011931197

PRINTED IN THE UNITED STATES OF AMERICA
on acid∞free paper

20 19 18 17 16 15 14 13 12 11   01 02 03 04 05 06 07 08 09 10

Chicken Soup for the Soul®

Devotional Stories for Tough Times

101 Daily Devotions to Inspire and Support You in Times of Need

Susan M. Heim
Karen C. Talcott
Foreword by Mary Beth Chapman

CSS

Chicken Soup for the Soul Publishing, LLC
Cos Cob, CT

Chicken Soup for the Soul

www.chickensoup.com

Contents

❶

~Lean on Me~

❷

~Be Strong and Courageous~

❸
~Surrender to God~

❹
~Power of Prayer~

❺

~Divine Signs~

❻

~His Healing Grace~

⑦

~Renewed Faith~

⑧

~Answered Prayers~

⑨

~Truth in the Word~

➓

~Count Your Blessings~

Foreword

March 26, 2011. Nearly three years of winter after losing our precious five-year-old, Maria Sue, as the result of an accident at our home. I was in the typical hurry-up mode of helping the two girls get out the door for school. Loading backpacks, gymnastics bags and anything else that needed to go, it was the typical ugly pile that happens when the Chapmans try to get to school on time.

As I walked around the back of the station wagon in my normal frenzied Mom mode, I was reminded of a recent visit to Target with Shaohannah, our now twelve-year-old. In the back window of the station wagon was a plastic container. It held nine stuffed flowers—the kind with long, green velvety stems and brightly colored petals. Each one had a smiley face placed right in the middle of the flower. Shaohannah had selected these strategically from the $1 section. Four bright orange flowers represented her dad, her brothers Caleb and Will Franklin, and Tanner, her sister Emily's husband. Three bright pink flowers represented Mom, Emily, and Julia, Caleb's wife. Two bright purple flowers represented Stevey Joy and herself. Then she spotted one of those big windmill things that you can stake in the ground and watch the wind whirl around. It was bright blue with a big ladybug stuck on it for a decorative touch. This would be chosen to represent our youngest, Maria, who is now in the arms of Jesus, making all of heaven a louder, more irresistible place.

On a normal day running errands, we were in Target, and it was time. The sun had been warming the air and softening the ground.

Winter seemed to be moving farther and farther in the distance, and its dark, short days had become longer, brighter ones. I watched Shaohannah carefully as she made her selections. Boy-colored flowers. Girl-colored flowers. She chose something a little bigger and special for Maria. She was very matter-of-fact and actually enjoyed the creativity and fun of making all of her selections.

On we went. Laundry detergent, toothpaste, cleaning supplies, snacks. You know the list—the one that never gets completely accomplished. "Mom," Shaoey said. "Look! It's a plaque that says 'WELCOME SPRING!' It's perfect to go with the flowers that I picked out." The spring-colored sign, hanging on the end of an aisle, was quickly and excitedly placed in the cart. We continued through Target until our list was mostly complete, then checked out and headed home.

On the way home, it struck me that whether we wanted to or not, we had welcomed spring! It had been a hard winter—one for me personally of wandering around a dark, ugly, snow-frozen forest, not sure which way to go to find my way out. I couldn't see, but knew I only had one option: Hold on to Jesus and have faith that He was with me every step of the journey. It was a huge step of faith, as tragedy had never been a part of my journey, and it took me to the bottom of my Christian faith. I had to choose to see that He was with me in the chaos of the terror that had stricken our family. I desperately needed to know that He was real. It was a choice. It was either all true or none of it was. I had a choice to make, and so I did. I held on to Jesus and began a painful, angry, and sometimes unbelieving walk through the forest, begging Him to help me in my unbelief, and to be the healer of my soul that He says He is.

Three years later, I would say that I'm now standing at the edge of that forest, but tempted to run back in, for that is what I've known for so long. I know that sounds odd, but though grief has become an unwelcome friend, it is nonetheless the friend I've known for a while now. Maria is there. The grief, the pain of losing her is there. Her memories are there. The good ones… There is only one horrific one: the day our spring turned to winter.

Then I see it. I feel the warmth, the sun. There, in front of me, is a beautiful field of daffodils, raising their delicate faces upward to their Creator as if they are praising Him for spring.

Thousands of daffodils are standing everywhere. Jesus is leading me, calling me ever so gently out of the forest, into the beautiful tapestry of flowers. I sense strongly that He is telling me it's time. It's time to run, play, live! He is reminding me that if He was with me in the dead forest, holding and literally carrying me on any given day, then He'll be with me in the playful flower fields of spring.

I'm scared. Leaving Maria? Leaving what has become all I know? Jesus nudges again… "You're not walking away from Maria, leaving her in the frozen darkness of where you've been. I, the Savior of your soul, am alive in you! In your heart! As you walk with me, you walk toward her! Death and pain are behind you, but life and joy are ahead. Maria is with me. I am with you. Maria will always be with you. As you journey this temporal life, remember that heaven is in front of you. You are walking toward eternity! I have her, she is safe, and you too will be with me soon. In the meantime, the little girl with the eyes that disappear when she smiles is right here on my lap, waiting for a hug from you that will never end."

Sometime this week, as spring in Tennessee continues to bloom and the flowers become more fragrant and colorful, the girls and I will drive to what we call Maria's spot. The memorial plaque will be cleaned of all the winter grime, and the vase will be emptied of the previous floral offerings that look as dead as the Tennessee winter days. We will arrange the stuffed flowers carefully and place the windmill gently in the center of it all. Then we will hold hands to pray and thank Jesus for the time that we had with Maria and remember the sweet, goofy times when our little Missy Moo made us laugh. "To infinity and beyond!" we'll say, declaring how much we love her. After that tearful yet grateful time, as we are ready to leave, we will gently hang the sign on the front of the brass vase that simply reads, "WELCOME SPRING."

"SEE! The winter is past; the rains are over and gone. Flowers appear on the earth; the season of singing has come…" (Song of Solomon 2:11-12).

I hope as you read through these devotions in *Chicken Soup for* the Soul: Devotional Stories for Tough Times, they will encourage you to keep on the journey toward spring. Whatever you have experienced that has caused winter to ascend and blanket your soul like snow covering a frozen lake will eventually lead you to a warm, flower-filled spring. Tough circumstances and grief take all of us on different journeys with similar characteristics. May you gain strength and be encouraged as you read stories about healing and encouragement that have been experienced by those who have walked through the cold, wintry forest and into the warm, flower-filled spring.

With hugs and gratitude,

~Mary Beth Chapman

New York Times Bestselling Author of
Choosing to SEE: A Journey of Struggle and Hope

Introduction

But I will sing of your strength, in the morning I will sing of your love; for you are my fortress, my refuge in times of trouble.
~Psalm 59:16

"*N*obody knows the troubles I've seen" is the first line in an old-time spiritual. How many times in your life have these words been in your heart? Probably more times than you can even remember. Tough times are a part of our life and spring up when we least expect them. They come in all sizes, shapes, and degrees of magnitude. But, regardless of how they occur, the problems in our life stop us in our tracks. Our lives are put on hold while we find ways to deal with our pain, humiliation, fear, grief, and even anger.

The Bible is filled with passages where God's people cry out for Him to hear their pain and ease their suffering. Psalm 116:1-4 is one such prayer to God. It reads, "*I love the Lord, for he heard my voice; he heard my cry for mercy. Because he turned his ear to me, I will call on him as long as I live. The cords of death entangled me, the anguish of the grave came upon me; I was overcome by trouble and sorrow. Then I called on the name of the Lord: 'O Lord, save me!'*"

As children of God, we want to know that God is real in tough times. Some fortunate people have a strong commitment to their faith, and tough times are just a bump in the road. But most of us struggle with our spiritual walk during the painful moments. We have a hard time holding onto the lifeline of the Holy Spirit. Like a drowning person, we look for anything or anybody who can help us through our pain. *Chicken Soup for the Soul: Devotional Stories for Tough Times* was written to be your source of comfort during your trials.

This book is filled with stories of men, women, and children who have been dealt a huge blow in their life. Some have lost a beloved child or loved one and can barely find the energy to make it through another day. Others are dealing with a financial hardship or job loss that threatens their family's fragile stability. And for many others, life has just thrown them a curveball, and they are merely trying to remain upright.

Yet, this book isn't only about tough times; it is also about hope. Psalm 116 continues (verses 5-7): *"The Lord is gracious and righteous, our God is full of compassion. The Lord protects the simplehearted; when I was in great need, he saved me. Be at rest once more, O my soul, for the Lord has been good to you."* This verse assures us of an amazing, wonderful, and eternal truth: God is with us, even during our struggles.

There are several ways in which you can read *Chicken Soup for the Soul: Devotional Stories for Tough Times*:

- **Start at the beginning!** Spend a little time with God each day by starting at the beginning of the book and reading a story each day for inspiration.

- **Pray for guidance.** Holding the book closed, pray for God to guide you to just the right devotional that you need to read that day. Randomly open the book and see where the Spirit leads!

- **Select a topic.** If you're dealing with a particular problem, scroll through the table of contents and turn to the appropriate chapter. Select a devotional that applies to your situation.

It is our wish that *Chicken Soup for the Soul: Devotional Stories for Tough Times* will inspire you and offer more proof that God walks with you during your moments of trial. We know that God's ever loving and guiding presence exists in each of these stories. Trust the wise scriptures, words, and prayers in this book, but more importantly, trust in Him. Let the God of Mercy gather you close, shielding you in His protective arms as you walk through tough times together.

~Susan and Karen

Will You Trust Me?

~Bonus Devotion~

By Mary Beth Chapman

How long, LORD? Will you forget me forever? How long will you hide your face from me? How long must I wrestle with my thoughts and day after day have sorrow in my heart? How long will my enemy triumph over me? Look on me and answer, LORD my God. Give light to my eyes, or I will sleep in death, and my enemy will say, "I have overcome him," and my foes will rejoice when I fall. But I trust in your unfailing love; my heart rejoices in your salvation. I will sing the LORD's praise, for he has been good to me.
~Psalm 13:1-6

*H*ave you ever found yourself in the "place" where the Psalmist was as he cried out this desperate prayer? Psalms like this one have become very precious to me as I have wrestled with my own thoughts and feelings of being "unloved," and wondering if and when God will come to my rescue.

I learned a little more about this prayer one night while trying to get our tiny Stevey Joy to swallow a tiny pill. Even at eight years old, she still has a very difficult time taking any kind of medicine in pill form. After trying for several minutes to no avail, and sensing myself growing frustrated, I "tagged" Dad and told him it was his turn to try. The longer Dad tried, the more upset both he and Stevey Joy became. He began to resort to all kinds of tactics, which resulted in more frustration. Finally, in desperation, she looked up at Steven and asked through her tears, "Daddy, don't you love me?" In other words, she was saying, "Daddy, if you love me, why would you be putting me through such misery and discomfort?"

In this moment, I could see myself in my little girl, looking up at her daddy and not able to understand why something so unpleasant, even scary and painful, would be allowed to come into my life. If God really loves me, why wouldn't He stop these hard providences from happening? Has He forgotten me? Will this sorrow in my heart ever go away? How long will my enemy be allowed to "triumph" over me like he seems to be doing in this moment? Does God really love me after all?

Steven tried to explain to Stevey Joy that not only did he and I love her very much, but even this thing that seemed so "unlovely"—like being made to take a pill—was in fact an act of love and for her good. Now it would be up to her to decide whether or not she would trust us.

In the same way, I can imagine all the times that we might pray or think those words, "God, don't you love me?" He responds with tears in His eyes, "More than you can imagine... So much that I gave my own Son to show how great my love is for you, and absolutely nothing can separate you from my love (Romans 8:38-39). 'I know the plans I have for you... plans to give you hope and a future' (Jeremiah 29:11). Now, will you trust me?"

When we find ourselves in those dark places like the Psalmist found himself in Psalm 13, crying out our questions and our pain to God, may the loudest cry of our heart be, "But I TRUST in your unfailing love... You have been good to me... I TRUST YOU!"

My Prayer

*Father, you ask us to place our trust in you, and
it should be so simple. Yet, so often when fear
and darkness invade our lives, we lose our ability
to clearly see you. Help us to find strength from
the mighty psalms and scriptures of your Word,
trusting that you are always with us, even while
we seek the answers to our questions.*

Amen.

Chapter

1

Devotional Stories for Tough Times

Lean on Me

Be completely humble and gentle;
be patient, bearing with one another in love.

~Ephesians 4:2

Angels Among Us

By Darlene Hierholzer

So do not fear, for I am with you; do not be dismayed, for I am your God.
I will strengthen you and help you;
I will uphold you with my righteous right hand.
~Isaiah 41:10

It was one o'clock in the morning when the call came, but I had already known for hours that he was gone. A mother knows when something has happened to her child. She feels it instinctively, in her bones. But as much as I didn't want to believe it, as much as I had been trying to convince myself that there was a logical explanation for why I wasn't able to reach my son, the police confirmed my worst nightmare.

I had to go to the impound lot to claim his car and empty it. It was the hardest thing I ever had to do. At first, I told myself I never wanted to see that car again. But after eight weeks, I needed to see and touch anything that belonged to him.

I started sobbing the moment his car came into view. Even from a distance, I could see the white sheet crumpled up on the seat, the exact place where my son had died. The lady who worked there must have seen my face and thought I might pass out because a second later she was by my side. She walked with me over to the car, and the first thing I saw were his sandals on the floor. They were left sitting up, as if he had just slipped his feet out of them. I reached down and grabbed them, feeling as though I was taking my son out of the car myself. I held the shoes close to my chest, and I felt the woman's arms around me, embracing me as my heart broke.

"I have a son, too," she said. "Lean on me."

That woman stayed with me, holding me up the entire time as I emptied the car. Her presence and her voice calmed me. Every time my knees grew a little wobbly, she'd whisper those three words again, "Lean on me."

I never got the woman's name, nor do I remember her face. All I remember is the compassion I saw in her eyes. I believe God sends people into our lives, instruments of His peace. And in that moment they act as angels, holding us up when we need them the most.

My Prayer

Sometimes in our lives we need to lean on others to make it through a difficult time. I thank you, Lord, that you send these sweet souls to us. They often show up without being called, but they help make our trials so much easier to bear.

Amen.

Angel at the Door

By Jeri McBryde

Do not be anxious about anything, but in every situation,
by prayer and petition, with thanksgiving, present your requests to God.
~Philippians 4:6

Angels have many names and shapes. The one who appeared at my family's door in July 2001 was my cousin, Casey.

Casey had no idea of the turmoil and anguish that was going on behind the door when he decided to visit us on that hot summer day. Having sold his business in Arizona, he was on a road trip, stopping here and there to visit relatives.

My sister and I were sobbing and praying. My mother, who had been my father's primary caregiver, had just been diagnosed with heart disease. She had an appointment with a specialist in two hours. What would happen now? Who should stay with my father? Who should take my mother to the hospital? Should we both go and take him with us? Our hearts were filled with confusion and doubt as we cried out to our Lord.

And then there was a knock on the door.

According to Casey, he had stopped at a motel to rest and plan the next step of his journey. "I had a dream last night," Casey said after we greeted him. "I kept seeing the shape of Tennessee and knew that I was needed."

He was at a crossroad that would change his life and enrich ours. One turn would take him to south-central Tennessee, the other to west Tennessee. He had relatives in both areas.

"When I came to the interstate exit, I found myself heading here."

What he didn't know was that my father had started his long, slow decline into Alzheimer's, and my mother was dying.

"Take your mother to the hospital, and I'll stay with your dad," Casey said as he unloaded his car.

My mother fought hard. My sister and I spent most of our time with her, comforted by the fact Casey was looking after my dad and the house. He cooked and cleaned. He built a deck with a wheelchair ramp and a walkway. But, most of all, he cared.

After three operations and four months, Mom's battle ended, and she went to be with our Lord. My father took my mother's death very hard. He refused to accept he had Alzheimer's, and the thought of leaving his home devastated him.

I was unable to quit my job. My sister had children to care for. One brother lived out of state, and the other had a job and family commitments. We were forced into looking at assisted-living homes despite his pleas to live at home.

We expected Casey to continue his journey. We were wrong.

"Don't worry," Casey assured my father. "I'll stay until the end."

And stay he did. For seven years, Casey took loving care of my father. But Casey did more; he gave us all comfort with his faith and belief in God's plans for our lives. He was an angel on Earth, and my family was blessed to have him.

My Prayer

*Thank you, dear Lord, for answering our prayers
and sending help to us in our time of need.
Continue to bless those who hear your word and
obey your commands. Let us all follow in the
footsteps of Jesus, who taught us the importance of
loving one another.*

Amen.

So Much to Live for

By Leslie Cooper

Blessed are those who have regard for the weak; the LORD delivers them in times of trouble. The LORD protects and preserves them—they are counted among the blessed in the land—he does not give them over to the desire of their foes. The LORD sustains them on their sickbed and restores them from their bed of illness.
~Psalm 41:1-3

The nurses would be changing shifts at 1:00 A.M. It would be the perfect time. No one would be around then. My son, Micah, had been hit by a truck three months prior. As a result, he had a severe head injury and was comatose. The doctors didn't expect him to live. If he did, they said he might never come out of the coma. I was heartbroken and couldn't stand to watch this happening to my son. He was twelve years old, an honor roll student, and very active in sports. He had a sense of humor that kept me laughing constantly. All of the girls were jealous of his big brown eyes and super-long eyelashes. He was smaller than most boys his age, and now he had lost so much weight and looked fragile. His father couldn't face it and wanted to institutionalize him. I disagreed, and we were headed for divorce. Finally, I told God that if He did not intervene, this would be the night. I went home, put my husband's 357 Magnum in my pocket, went back to the hospital, and waited for

1:00. I would kill Micah and then myself. Surely, God didn't expect our lives to go on this way.

About five minutes later, I was surprised to see a middle-aged man roll into the room in a wheelchair. Our nurse, Ellen, introduced him as Ricardo, one of the chaplains. She said she would sit with Micah so we could go down the hall to another room. Then he began to tell me the story about when he had been injured ten years ago. As he lay paralyzed in the hospital in a semi-comatose state, he could hear all of the conversations going on around him and knew the prognosis wasn't good. As the nurses brought in syringes of morphine every day and laid them on his nightstand, he would take one with the one arm he could still move and place it under his mattress. When he had acquired enough of them, he would inject himself and be done with this life. No one knew that he could move one arm and they didn't think he was cognitive, so they never suspected him.

One night, he decided to watch an ongoing series called *Hill Street Blues*. It was so interesting that he wanted to see what happened next, even though it meant waiting one more week to kill himself. For the next two weeks, the same thing happened. Finally, he thought, "If this show could make me want to live, there has to be much more to live for." So, he decided to live.

Years later, Micah is still alive. Although he is a quadriplegic and cognitively three years old, he is happy and at peace. One day, when Micah had to be hospitalized again, Ricardo came by. I asked if he remembered when he told me the *Hill Street Blues* story, and he answered yes, but he had no idea I was planning murder and suicide that night. I explained how I had told God that if He didn't intervene, I would kill my son and myself. As Ricardo listened, tears ran down his face. He said, "You are not going to believe this, but only minutes ago I told God that unless He intervened, I was going to quit my job here because I didn't believe I was making a difference. And then you told me your story." We both looked over at Micah, and he smiled at us as if to say, "All is as it should be because God wanted us to know that there is so much to live for."

My Prayer

Dear God, grant us the ability to realize that we can't make decisions according to how we feel or by what we think we want. We need to prayerfully consider all the options before we act on our impulses. We are blessed that you are a God who hears our thoughts and intervenes before we proceed with our plans.

Amen.

4

More Than Cookies and Kool-Aid

By Carolyn K. Knefely

Above all, love each other deeply, because love covers over a multitude of sins.
Offer hospitality to one another without grumbling.
~1 Peter 4:8-9

I don't even remember their names, the ladies who made the greatest impact in my life. However, I took to heart what they taught with their blue felt storyboards. These ladies fed me more than cookies and Kool-Aid. They showed their love for Jesus Christ by feeding me, an abandoned, abused, and rejected lamb.

Our stepmother locked us kids out of the house each morning all summer. My little brothers and I heard the same song, "Don't you kids come back until it's dark!" How I wished the song was, "Breakfast is ready," but it never happened. Instead, I learned to steal a lump of brown sugar before being pushed out the door at dawn.

My brothers and I were first in line waiting for the church doors to open since we had already played a couple of hours in the park on the merry-go-round, swings, and teeter-totters. Smelly and dirty, we would wait for the perfumed ladies to unlock the doors. Their friendly smiles were a welcome sight. They always said, "Come in!"

Being street-smart scavengers, we were quick to learn to sit, wait, and watch. Listening to the ladies' stories was a real treat, right up there with the sweet treats. How nice it was not to be chased away, but accepted.

The storyboards showed us that Jesus loved children, and He fed people. It seemed to this six-year-old that his favorite foods were fish and bread. He made baskets full to share. I liked fish and bread. I hadn't tasted much love until that day on a wet mattress.

It was a dreary day when my stepmother put my wet mattress in the front yard. Since I was a bed wetter, she seemed to want the neighbors to see what a bad girl I was. With a childish thought, I climbed up on the wet mattress to show the neighbors that my new mother was being nice so I could take a nap outside. Silently, I added tears to the puddled pad because of what she screamed when she saw me lying there.

"I can see why your mom left you and never came back. I tried to give you to her sisters and parents. They don't want you. I don't want you. Nobody wants you."

As tears slid down to the stained and dingy mattress, I looked up and prayed, "God, no one wants me. Let me be your little girl." The church ladies had told us God loved children.

Life changed for me over the years because my Heavenly Father took me from a dirty castaway to a lady of dignity, teaching fine-dining etiquette and how to build meaningful relationships through simple hospitality. He made me His little girl that day on a wet mattress.

The journey of change began with those perfumed women whose names I can't remember. They touched my life with acceptance, care, and real food. God has not forgotten their names.

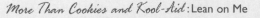

My Prayer

Thank you, God, for wonderful people who
answer the call to share your love with children.
Jesus valued children and their place in the
kingdom of heaven. May we realize that these
tiny ears and hearts are waiting to be nourished,
and we all have an important part to play
in their upbringing.

Amen.

"I love the cookies and
Kool-Aid... but I'll take
a second helping of
God's love!"

Reprinted by permission of
Stephanie Piro ©2011.

Lessons from Matt

By Peggy Purser Freeman

"The King will reply, 'Truly I tell you, whatever you did for one of the least of these brothers and sisters of mine, you did for me.'"
~Matthew 25:40

"Just what am I doing in a place like this?" I had turned down this job assignment two years before, but now it was this job, as an aide in the school for the severe and profoundly disabled, or no job. This was the oldest building in the district. The walls reeked with fifty years of sweat, vomit, and vermin odor. It had been one of the city's most beautiful facilities; now it warehoused those whom some administrators wanted out of sight and out of mind.

The small bathroom smelled of urine and human waste. The hard tile floor cut into my knees. I slung the jeans I had just pulled off the thin, braced legs of my nine-year-old charge and grumbled aloud.

"I wanted to write songs and stories for you, God."

I had spent most of my three weeks at this job with Matt, trying to get him to go to the bathroom on the potty, put a block in a can or at least make eye contact. To get him to look me in the eyes proved to be the most difficult. His eyes seemed to be the only thing he was able to control. He had no verbal skills, little motor control. All he had was the ability to look away or squeeze his eyes shut, anything but eye contact.

As I took the soiled underwear off Matt to clean his legs and bottom, I dropped the feces-covered underwear on my dress. "Oh, Matt, look what you've done!" I screamed.

He gave his soundless laugh and smiled a grin made toothless from the many falls his wobbly legs had taken. Most days that smile would have melted my heart, but not today. My love was stretched thin, and my patience broke. "God, I hate this."

The small room grew still, and I felt Matt's stare. I glanced up and met his eyes. Large and luminous, they looked into mine, staring into my soul. In the quietness of the moment, I heard words with my heart — not Matt's voice and not mine.

"I didn't ask you to rewrite Sunday school literature. I didn't ask you to write songs. I said if you do it unto the least of these, you've done it unto me." Then Matt looked away.

God spoke to my heart in a most profound way in that smelly bathroom. In the years that followed, I learned to listen, and Matt taught me so many things. You don't have to be capable of seesawing to sit on one and enjoy white clouds in a blue sky. Soundless laughter and silent tears often communicate better than words. Life in its most simple form is sometimes life at its best. Probably the best lesson I learned: God talks the loudest through the weakest.

My Prayer

*Father God, thank you for allowing us to meet
your needs by doing for others. Forgive us for
not seeing immediately the plans you have for
us—even when the plans are not those we would
choose. Help us to listen and to search for you in
all situations. Thank you for the people in our life
who become great teachers.*

Amen.

Chicken Soup for the Soul

The Line-Up

By Rita Billbe

They all wept as they embraced him and kissed him.
~Acts 20:37

Three days after funeral services for my nineteen-year-old son, Shawn, I debated the wisdom of watching a baseball game. My normal job responsibilities as high school principal included attending athletic events. This duty proved exhausting, especially in the spring when numerous activities also claimed my calendar. But this was different. Regional play-offs included our baseball team, and normally I would have been excited. But I wasn't sure I could tolerate the sight of all those teenage "hard bodies" playing for their shot at number one, a trophy forever lost to my young athlete.

Sitting in my dreary duplex, almost drowning in despair, I craved normalcy. The day before, we'd chosen a gravestone marker, and the process almost broke me. My tears simply wouldn't stop, and today would be no better if I didn't move forward. Maybe leaving my recliner to feel the sun on my face would spark some energy where there was none.

I managed to move the car from the garage and headed to the field. On the way, I reminisced about this team. They had been hard-headed, cocky, and prone to disciplinary problems. But we had finally managed a peaceful co-existence, and I was proud of them. I arrived at the stadium, found some of my colleagues, and sat behind them. Somehow, we fumbled through our greetings. Their woebegone faces portrayed their shock, their empathy, and finally admiration that I had come. We watched the game with easy familiarity and without the need to carry on long conversations.

Our team didn't perform well. Their score remained low, and their enthusiasm and efforts notwithstanding, they simply couldn't overcome a stronger, more competent squad.

Feeling the last threads of my composure begin to unravel, I said goodbyes to my staff, moved toward the parking lot, and called out "good game" to a few boys as they left the dugout. Just as I exited the gate, however, I heard a murmuring of my name. I stopped and turned around. At that moment, the entire team lined up outside the gate, came forward one at a time, and hugged me. As only teenage boys could do, they expressed themselves in their own way.

Suddenly, I realized the gift God had bestowed. Their warm embraces reminded me of Shawn's. Just as I did when hugging his six-foot frame, I had to stand on tiptoe to reach some of them. They didn't rush. No one jostled the other or told anyone to hurry up. They simply gave the gift of a teenage boy's presence to a mother who craved one.

To this day, I can picture the sight of those dirty uniforms, the smell of sweat and fear accompanied by smiles and loving faces. I don't remember the score or who we played or even a single name of our players. But I'll never forget that line-up.

My Prayer

God, thank you for the comfort you send us from the most unexpected places. Even though our grief seems unbearable, you find loving ways to lift our spirits. And if we are lucky enough, we might even catch a tiny glimpse of heaven.

Amen.

A Beautiful Mess

By Diane Stark

Therefore encourage one another and build each other up,
just as in fact you are doing.
~1 Thessalonians 5:11

"He left me," I whispered into the phone. "He said he didn't love me anymore."

"Oh, sweetheart, I'm so sorry," my stepfather, Doug, said. "Your mom and I are here for you. Whatever you need, you can count on us."

When my mother's husband made that promise, I'm sure he didn't realize how much it would involve. I'm sure he didn't plan on having his stepdaughter and her two young children move in with him. But it happened, and he was wonderful about it.

I should have been grateful, but I was too wrapped up in my own pain to notice the sacrifices others were making. I cried a lot and ate next to nothing. Sadly, I abdicated much of my parenting responsibilities to my mom and Doug.

Shortly after moving in, I began to find little notes on my dresser. But they weren't from my mom; they were from Doug. My favorite one read, "If you ever need a shoulder to cry on, the Lord gave me two of them. They're big and strong, and they're available anytime you need them."

I went downstairs and made good use of that shoulder. When I'd finally stopped crying, Doug said, "What's the hardest part of this for you?"

I shrugged. "My life is a mess."

"You may see a mess, but God sees it as an opportunity for growth. He's molding your heart and drawing you to Him. It may be a mess, but it's a beautiful one."

I was definitely a mess, but there was nothing beautiful about it.

In the silence, Doug added, "God isn't nearly as concerned with where we've come from as He is with where we're going. And you're heading in the right direction, honey."

I muttered a thank-you and went back upstairs.

Two days later, I found a small plaque in my room. It read, "God gave you 86,400 seconds today. Have you used one of them to say thank you?"

I wanted to ignore the little sign. I wanted to say, "Thank Him for what? My life is a mess, remember?" But I couldn't. I couldn't deny the evidence that God still loved me. I still had my children, and we had a roof over our heads and food to eat. Despite everything, we were okay. And God was there—I could feel Him. He loved me. He'd never left me, and He never would.

Sobbing, I got down on my knees and thanked God for the beautiful mess my life had become. I thanked Him for His love and His faithfulness to my children and me. But most of all, I thanked Him for a man named Doug, who had become so much more than just my mother's husband. For all his patience and persistence, Doug was now my second dad.

My Prayer

Thank you, Lord, for sending the right people into our lives just when we need them most. Thank you for blessing us with such wonderful friends and family. Help us to encourage and build up one another, especially in times of trouble.

Amen.

Six Little Words

By Robin A. Bridges

"'Love your neighbor as yourself.'"
~Mark 12:31

*D*earest Stranger,

I write this story because our paths may never meet again. If they do intersect, it is likely I will not recognize you, and it is equally probable you will not recognize me. Our paths crossed for a mere five seconds—not long enough to take in the details of your face, the color of your hair, or even the make and model of your car with any certainty. But for that blink of time, during those few seconds that it took for the traffic signal to turn from red to green, you profoundly impacted my life, and I will always remember you as the stranger who loves me.

Yes, LOVE. It is a strange word to use when talking about a stranger. But that is exactly what I felt flow from your heart and into mine as I sat gripping the steering wheel, tears streaming down my face, wondering how I would live my life with the horribly painful empty space that was growing wider and deeper every second as my father, my best friend, slipped away from me forever. I could not imagine life without him. How could I go on living and not talk to him, hear his laughter, or share a cup of coffee on the porch, which was our daily routine? It was too hard, too excruciating. I was not strong enough to say goodbye. Yet, it was his time, and God was calling Dad home. So I sat there at that light, white-knuckled and trembling, with tears pouring from my eyes.

That is when I met you, the loving stranger in the left lane, with the kind eyes and gentle voice. You did not know me or what I was crying about, but you could feel my pain and wanted to do something to make it better. I may not know your name or remember what you look like, but I will always remember your words, "You have a good day, okay?" Six little words, a simple sentence — such a little thing that you may not even remember it. But for me they meant the world, expressed with warmth, concern, and genuine love from one human being to another. Those words gave me the strength I needed to drive to the hospital that day and see my dad through his final hours.

I have no doubt that when I had no strength, God delivered you, a stranger with a heart full of love, to lift me up and pull me through. So, when I reflect back to this trying time, I am thankful for God, my family, and YOU. I thank you with all my heart. I will always remember those six little words and what they did for me that day — and still do today.

Eternally yours,
Stranger

My Prayer

*Dear Lord, thank you for sending loving people
to help us through the hardest times in our lives.
May we always remember their simple acts of
kindness and how their words, no matter how few,
give us the strength to go on. I pray, Lord Jesus,
that you will help me bless someone else with
my words and my presence when they are going
through a tough time.*

Amen.

The Child Who Never Came

By Susan M. Heim

My comfort in my suffering is this: Your promise preserves my life.
~Psalm 119:50

After just two months of "trying," I got great news: I was pregnant! I was absolutely thrilled. But because I knew that the first three months of pregnancy could be delicate, I told only my closest family members and my boss. I experienced a little morning sickness, but it stopped around seven weeks. I was so lucky! Everything was going beautifully. At the end of my twelfth week, I decided it was time to share the news at work. We were having a staff meeting, so I chose that time to make the announcement. Everyone was delighted for me. After I left the meeting, I went into the ladies' room. There I discovered a heartbreaking sight: blood. I was losing the baby.

An ultrasound revealed that the baby had only developed to seven weeks—the very same time when my morning sickness went away. I was devastated. Not surprisingly, I struggled with the reasons for my miscarriage. I hadn't touched a drop of alcohol or caffeine. I'd taken my prenatal vitamins and avoided pesticides and harsh cleaning products. I'd taken such good care of myself and my baby. But the child wasn't meant to be, and I couldn't understand why God had let this happen.

Meanwhile, my co-workers gathered around me. I discovered that four out of the five women with whom I worked directly had miscarried at one point. All four had gone on to have successful pregnancies. The fifth woman struggled with infertility but later happily adopted. These women understood the pain I felt at losing my child, and were able to comfort me during the times when I just wanted to curl up under the covers and not face the world.

I will never know why my first baby died, but I thank God for surrounding me with friends who knew exactly how I was feeling. With no family around, my co-workers became a safe port during a very rocky time in my life. I felt God's presence through their kind words and actions. They carried my burden when I feared I could no longer do so. And I will be forever grateful for the strength of their arms, which could only have come from our Father.

My Prayer

*Dear God, give us the courage to share our
sorrows when they threaten to overwhelm us.
Please bring people into our lives who can share
the tremendous love you freely give to us all.
May we recognize your presence in the faces of
those around us.*

Amen.

10

The Grand Canyon Angel

By Maria Norris

"See, I am sending an angel ahead of you to guard you along the way…"
~Exodus 23:20

I once thought that if I ever saw an angel, he would appear in a blaze of celestial light—a magnificent creature with flowing hair and outstretched wings. He'd carry a mighty sword, and his arrival would be announced by a thundering fanfare. Never did I imagine that "my" angel would be an unassuming fellow in shorts, knee socks, and hiking boots. But his appearance left me every bit as awestruck as if he had been the Archangel Michael himself in all his glory.

My encounter with this heavenly being occurred several years ago in Arizona. I was vacationing at the South Rim of the Grand Canyon with my parents, aunt, and uncle. It was a beautiful summer day, and we were hiking the Rim Trail that runs from Grand Canyon Village to Hermit's Rest. After an easy 1.4-mile walk along the wide, paved path, we reached Maricopa Point. From there on, the trail is unpaved, narrow, and sometimes perilously close to the edge. Beckoned by the scenic piñon-juniper woodland and lack of crowds, we decided to continue along the meandering dirt trail a little way before turning around and heading back to the Village.

We went single file, with my fit, seventy-three-year-old dad leading the way. He had just rounded a bend in the trail when he lost his footing in some loose gravel and started to slide off the edge of the cliff. Fortunately, he was able to break his fall by grabbing onto the branch of a scrub pine growing just below the rim, but unfortunately he was too far out of reach for any of us to help him. My uncle lay flat on his stomach and somehow managed to grab Dad's hand. But my uncle wasn't strong enough to pull him up; rather, it seemed more likely that my dad would pull him down—over the edge. So there they were, my uncle and my dad, dangling 5,000 feet above the floor of the Grand Canyon with three helpless females in a panic, not knowing what to do—and no one else in sight.

Then, seemingly out of nowhere, a man appeared on the path whistling some nameless tune. With his graying hair sticking out from beneath a white fishing cap and knobby knees visible below a pair of Bermuda shorts, he looked like an eccentric, aging college professor. It took him only a second to assess the situation, and without saying a word and barely breaking stride, he reached into the abyss with a long, sinewy arm and plucked my dad and uncle from the brink of death as if they weighed no more than a feather. Still whistling, he continued on his way, leaving us astounded as well as profoundly relieved and grateful.

We all knew something miraculous had just happened. What that mysterious stranger had done didn't seem humanly possible. Was he truly an angel? Maybe. Or maybe not. Regardless, he was truly heaven-sent.

My Prayer

*God of the ages, thank you for reminding us that
we never travel alone. We are part of you always.
Thank you for the miracles that occur in our life
as answers to our prayers.*

Amen.

Chapter
2

Devotional Stories for Tough Times

Be Strong and Courageous

… we went through fire and water,
but you brought us to a place of abundance.

~Psalm 66:12

On His Knees

By Teresa Ambord

In my distress I called to the LORD; I cried to my God for help.
From his temple he heard my voice; my cry came before him, into his ears.
~Psalm 18:6

My dad probably never envisioned becoming a husband and father by the time he was nineteen. That was a lot of responsibility, but it was nothing compared to what was to come. Leap forward eleven years, and he and Mom had four daughters. With their combined incomes, my parents bought a big, new house. We moved in, but just a few months later, their marriage fell apart, and Mom moved out. That meant Dad not only had to raise four daughters alone, but he also had to pay for a two-income house with one income.

Becoming a suddenly single parent is always a struggle, but much more so for a man trying his best to raise girls. As in most families, Mom had done most of the nurturing. Dad knew little about cooking and less about housework. He hired babysitters and housekeepers, always with disastrous results. So, in the end, the five of us winged it. In the morning, I'd walk myself to school across the street. After school, I'd walk home and wait in the garage till my older sisters got home. I never told them that I was afraid to go into a house that had been empty all day.

Long after dark, Dad would arrive home. He was exhausted from ten-hour days, and though I didn't realize it then, he was also deeply troubled by the breakup with Mom. Even so, every night after work, he'd stop to spend time with us. We'd crawl all over him and tell him the complaints we'd waited to lodge against each other.

After a while, Dad would stand up and say, "Girls, I just need a few quiet minutes," and then he'd disappear into his bedroom.

Soon, we would start quarreling amongst ourselves, and we'd look around for our chief problem-solver.

"Dad!" we'd scream almost in unison. Then we'd burst into his room to tattle, and always find Dad kneeling by his bed in prayer. Those chaotic days are a blur now, but seeing Dad on his knees, humbling himself before God, is a sight I will never forget. His world had turned upside-down, draining his energy, but he knew where to go to renew his strength. He knew it was God who equipped him to get through another day as the suddenly single father of four. Whether he realized it then or not, he was also setting an example for his daughters.

These days, if I run out of strength, I remember where to go to renew the supply. There's a saying, "When times get tough, the tough get on their knees." Like my dad, I get on my knees, and I feel restored.

My Prayer

Heavenly Father, I know that when my heart breaks, I can come to you to put it back together again, in your way and in your time. Help draw me near to you so I may listen to your voice of assurance that you whisper into my heart.

Amen.

12

Chicken Soup for the Soul

Truth at the Benefit Sale

By David Ozab

Hear my prayer, LORD; listen to my cry for mercy.
When I am in distress, I call to you, because you answer me.
~Psalm 86:6-7

"Cleft lip."

The words had rung in my head since the ultrasound. At twenty-two weeks, a shadow on our unborn child's lip shattered our dreams of the perfect baby. We were facing surgeries, possible feeding problems, and other unknown complications. How were we going to handle this? We prayed every night, desperate for an answer, but the question still haunted us. After two weeks of anguish, we needed a break.

That's why Julia suggested we go to this benefit sale. It was for a six-month-old boy born with a hole in his heart, and as helpless as we felt, we still wanted to help someone else.

We started at opposite ends of the driveway, sorting through tables crowded with clothes and toys. As we met in the middle, Julia picked up a puppet. "Isn't this cute?"

"Do we need another animal?" We own a lot of stuffed animals.

"It's a puppet. We only have a few puppets."

"Well, we're gonna buy something, and he is adorable."

We handed the puppet to the woman at the cash table.

"Oh, that's precious." She checked the price. "Two dollars."

Julia handed her a twenty. "Consider the rest a donation."

The woman's eyes filled with tears. "Oh, God bless you. Are you sure you don't want something else?"

We glanced at each other.

"I'll take one more look," Julia said. "We may have missed something."

As she browsed, a man walked up to the table holding a baby clad in a striped blue shirt and denim overalls.

"Somebody wants to say 'hi.'"

The woman took her baby boy into her arms. At that moment, I saw that he had Down syndrome—as if dealing with heart surgeries wasn't enough.

Julia returned to the cash table with a baby blanket in time for introductions.

"Hi, Noah," we said.

He replied with a glimmering, cherubic smile.

"He's got such an incredible spirit given everything he's been through."

His mother lifted his shirt, revealing a jagged scar that ran like a fault line from his neck to his navel. He giggled as she tickled him, which made us all laugh.

She pulled his shirt back down and cradled him on her shoulder. "It's been harder on us, watching him go through two surgeries and knowing he's got more ahead of him."

I couldn't imagine what she and her husband were going through. I thought about our baby's cleft surgery. It didn't seem as overwhelming anymore.

As we drove away, I could tell that Julia felt as hopeful as I did. Neither of us spoke for several minutes. We each knew what the other was thinking, but Julia put it into words: "With God's help, we can handle this, too."

My Prayer

*God, our Father, you are always with us, even
at our darkest moments, and you answer our
prayers in ways we never expect. Hear us now,
we beseech you, and give us the help we need to
bear the trials of our earthly pilgrimage. This we
ask through Jesus Christ our Lord.*

Amen.

13

The Christmas Ornament

By Karen Asire

You make known to me the path of life; you will fill me with joy in your presence, with eternal pleasures at your right hand.
~Psalm 16:11

As the children excitedly opened the box of Christmas ornaments and began hanging them on the tree, I struggled to keep back the tears. I had dreaded this moment, keenly aware of the painful memories it would bring back. In some ways, it seemed like just yesterday that we had packed away the Christmas decorations and, in other ways, it was more like an eternity. The past year had certainly brought many changes to our lives. It was now four months since my husband announced he was leaving, and a divorce loomed in the coming year. The hurt was almost unbearable, but with three young children, I hid my tears as often as possible and kept going. Today was one of those days when the tears would have to wait until after they were asleep. As they continued to decorate the tree, I secretly set aside several ornaments, including one that said "Our First Christmas Together."

Several days later, a knock was heard at the door. As I opened it, our neighbor handed me an ornament. "We've hung this ornament on our tree for several years, but this year we wanted you to have it for your tree," she said. I glanced at the beautiful gold ornament and was surprised to see it spelled the word JOY. I thanked her and hung the ornament on our tree.

As I stood back and looked at the tree, all the other ornaments seemed to fade into the background, and all I saw was the shimmering gold of the JOY ornament. The tears began to fall as I silently thanked God for this reminder. In the midst of grief and heartache, He promises to be with us. God's presence brings a joy that circumstances cannot take away. Although several ornaments were missing from our tree that year, I realized they would be replaced with new ones. Each ornament would come with a new memory, and the pain of the past would gradually fade.

Many Christmases have passed since that year. God has truly brought much joy into my life. There have been other heartaches along the way, but each year the JOY ornament hangs on our Christmas tree as a reminder of God's unfailing love.

My Prayer

Father, thank you for the peace you give, even in the midst of heartache. Thank you for making yourself known to us in difficult times. With a joyful heart, I know that nothing in this lifetime can ever shake your unfailing love for me.

Amen.

" That's just what we needed this year, Mom. Let's make Joy a family tradition!"

Reprinted by permission of
Stephanie Piro ©2011.

More Than Many Sparrows

By Sue Tornai

Are not two sparrows sold for a penny?
Yet not one of them will fall to the ground outside your Father's care...
So don't be afraid; you are worth more than many sparrows.
~Matthew 10:29-31

Panic flooded my soul. *This can't be happening,* I said to myself. I looked for one last severance pay deposit when I checked my account online, but was shocked when it wasn't there. I wondered how I would pay the phone bill.

I had felt indispensable at my job. The volume of work, and the daily, weekly, and monthly deadlines made me crazy. Then, one day, my supervisor asked me for help. Eagerly, I followed her into the conference room. She closed the door behind us. "This has nothing to do with your performance," my boss said.

"Okay," I said. Thoughts of the market crash six months earlier, the past year of downsizing, and the increased number of empty offices passed through my mind. I wondered if my job was on the line.

The office manager made a conference call to the home office and then read a letter to me, confirming my fear—my job had been eliminated. She explained the details of my termination while I froze in my chair.

"Are you all right?" my boss asked.

"Yes," I said. What was I supposed to say?

"Take the afternoon off, Sue, and read over this material," she said, handing me a stack of folders describing my benefits and severance. "I'll see you tomorrow."

Bewildered, I drove home that day feeling helpless and worthless. I wondered what I would say to my husband. During the weeks and months that followed, applications for work brought few interviews, and the interviews didn't bring job offers. Now, several months later, my severance pay was gone.

Leaving the house for my morning walk, a cool breeze blew through my hair, and I sensed God was near. The fresh scent of flowers and the beauty of the tree-lined streets beckoned me. Praying as I walked, I saw a flock of sparrows fly overhead and then perch on a nearby fence. It seemed as if I heard Jesus say, "Are not two sparrows sold for a penny? Yet not one of them will fall to the ground outside your Father's care… So don't be afraid; you are worth more than many sparrows" (Matthew 10:29-31).

Could God love me that much? Enough to send sparrows? How could I worry about the phone bill? How could I forget what God had done for me in other uncertain times? His amazing love gave me hope, and my unemployment check came just in time to pay the phone bill.

Now when I am tempted by fear or feelings of failure, I remember the sparrows and Jesus's words. I'm still unemployed, but I don't feel worthless. Instead, I help those who are employed by volunteering at church or taking my grandchildren to school after my daughter leaves for work. The sparrows reminded me how God has taken care of me in the past, and I trust He will take care of me now.

My Prayer

*Thank you, Lord, for being involved in my life
and giving me hope. I find peace in knowing
that you will never leave me alone to battle my
insecurities and fear. I trust you for all my needs
now and in the future.*

Amen.

Running Soles

By Christina D'Agostino

Therefore I do not run like someone running aimlessly…
~1 Corinthians 9:26

My senior year at Mount Saint Mary's University is ending. The future waits with endless possibilities. My feet glide along the road as I enjoy the company of my running partner and friend, Elizabeth DiNunzio. My thoughts drift to the future, and my stomach battles the unnerving feeling of beginning a new chapter in my life. Restlessly, I confide in Liz, "I'm nervous to start teaching." The road bends upward, and she confidently embraces the path before her. With her glistening smile and uplifting words, she reassures me and eases my concern. Finishing a run with Liz leaves me with a feeling of accomplishment and sets my day in motion.

A few days later, Liz's life tragically comes to an end when a careless driver stops the melody of her running feet days before her first marathon and graduation. An insurmountable sadness weighs on my heart.

My stirring mind futilely tries to unravel the mystery of God's plan. I know her radiant smile and kind heart would have been a blessing to her future students. The world needed Liz. Tears cloud my vision as I pray for comfort.

Fueled by a sense of loss, I lace up my sneakers in a search for answers. For her, I need to run a marathon and teach my students the beauty of their dreams.

The physical pain of running helps to numb the emotional pain of loss. I challenge my body with each climbing hill and take the road before me in stride. An inner strength disciplines each run. While running, I listen to the whispering wind rustling the cornstalks and ask for healing.

On the eve of my first marathon, feelings of self-doubt and confusion escalate. Each repetitive beat of the second hand pierces my ears as I wrestle the night. I pray, "God, be with me. I do not want to run alone."

Then a peaceful serenity comes over me as flashbacks illuminate the night. Like a videotape set to replay, I vividly relive my runs with Liz. A shard of light peaks through the window curtains, and I rise and face the twenty-six miles ahead of me.

While running, a black sign etched in gold letters reads "Run Elizabeth." Her Pittsburgh spirit runs through me, and an instantaneous runner's high soars through my body. It is this same spirit that empowers me during my first year of teaching.

The journey of twenty-six miles leads me back to my classroom. The smiling faces and eager minds of my students jog my memory back to my first day of teaching. My once flip-flopping stomach rests easy. My eyes open, and I see students with endless dreams, ambitions, and possibilities.

My Prayer

Lord, when life leaves me filled with fear,
And I am afraid because the future is near,
Run with me and make the direction clear.

Amen.

Chicken Soup for the Soul

Rain in the Pond

By Crystal Brennan Ruzicka

Then he got into the boat and his disciples followed him. Suddenly a furious
storm came up on the lake, so that the waves swept over the boat. But Jesus
was sleeping. The disciples went and woke him, saying, "Lord, save us! We're
going to drown!" He replied, "You of little faith, why are you so afraid?" Then
he got up and rebuked the winds and the waves, and it was completely calm.
~Matthew 8:23-26

I should have known better. I did know better, in fact, and I told
myself as I balanced two bowls of cereal and a glass of juice
between my fingers that it was a really bad idea.

I felt them slip milliseconds before they fell. No time to do anything but watch everything smash onto the floor, spilling milk, juice,
and broken glass across the kitchen. I remember screaming as I ham-
mered my fist against the side of the refrigerator.

My four-year-old daughter and one-year-old son were patiently
waiting for breakfast. Hot tears rained down my face as I wondered
how to explain to them that there was nothing else to eat. We were
dead broke. Paycheck to paycheck didn't describe our life; it was
more like paycheck to three days before the next paycheck. Those
bowls of cereal and that glass of juice represented more than breakfast. I'd been so proud of the fact that I'd rationed our groceries so

that we had just enough food to last until my husband came home with his check.

So when I cried, the tears were for so much more than the mess.

"It's okay, Mommy," my daughter said quietly. I turned to her, wiping my eyes as I thought of how to explain how not okay it was. "It's all just rain in the pond, Mommy," she continued, her wide eyes shining with understanding.

The power behind those words struck me profoundly. What's one storm to a pond? Nothing. It might seem like a big deal in that moment, but when the clouds part, the big pond sits unchanged.

I had no idea what was coming down the road. I didn't know that my sweet boy who called me Mama and giggled through peek-a-boo games was going to lose his voice to a monster called autism. I didn't know that my world was going to seem so dark as I fought for my son, that the blackness would threaten to consume me.

But thanks to my daughter, I did know this: No matter how awful those storms felt when I was standing within them, they would pass. I might be different after passing through them, but the core of who I am as a child of God would be unchanged. And I would never weather them alone.

My Prayer

Lord, we know waves will crash through our lives.
You have the power to protect us when our boat
feels like it is capsizing. Thank you for reminding
us that difficult times are just
raindrops in the pond.

Amen.

No Regrets

By Lindy Schneider

The Lord Himself goes before you and will be with you; He will never leave
you nor forsake you. Do not be afraid; do not be discouraged.
~Deuteronomy 31:8

"Live your life so you have no regrets." Those were my mom's words. It was her life motto, and I tried to live that way as well. No regrets means telling the people I love how important they are to me. It means apologizing when I am wrong. But, most importantly, no regrets means being there for the people who need me.

With four kids, "being there" was a full-time job. My husband and I spent our Saturdays attending baseball and soccer games. We were determined to watch every high school play and church drama in which the kids played a role. During the weekdays, between cooking, shopping, and my part-time job, I chauffeured the kids and their friends to their many activities. I met dates at the door and teachers at the school. It was a simple matter of carefully scheduling around responsibilities each week to make sure I would be there for my family. It was simple, that is, until my mom began to need me more than usual.

In her seventies, Mom was diagnosed with Alzheimer's disease. She needed quite a bit of supervision, so I began to pick her up daily, and we accomplished my to-do list together. For a while, she integrated into the family activities very well. However, as the disease progressed, all the people and places became too much for her, and I had to stop bringing her along on my many errands and routines.

We found an assisted-living community for Mom, and I began to drop some of what I was doing for my family to spend time with just her. Mom gradually lost her memory of who I was, but her face always brightened when she saw me. We would walk together and sometimes sing. Although Mom was in the hands of excellent care-givers, tears would run down my face whenever I drove away from our visit.

"Lord," I prayed, "Mom needs me so much, but I need to be home for my family, too. How can I be everywhere?" I was wracked with guilt and exhaustion, feeling like I was disappointing everyone. I regretted each time I left Mom to take care of my family's needs, and I regretted leaving my family to spend time with her. As I quietly wept, a thought came across my heart. I knew it was God speaking to me: "I didn't create you to be everywhere; I am everywhere. I am omnipresent."

The peace of understanding began to trickle into my aching heart. My prayers changed from "How can I be everywhere?" to "Thank you, Lord, that you are with my loved ones always, even when I can't be there." The weeks continued to be hectic, and I did my best to accommodate all the needs, but I no longer had to just let some things go. Instead, I gave them to Jesus, and I've never regretted that.

My Prayer

*Lord Jesus, thank you that you know my
limitations. Thank you that my responsibilities
are not mine alone. You are with me and with my
loved ones always. Help me to rest in you.*

Amen.

No Matter What

By Michelle Close Mills

"'But I will rescue you on that day, declares the LORD; you will not be given into the hands of those you fear. I will save you; you will not fall by the sword but will escape with your life, because you trust in me, declares the LORD.'"
~Jeremiah 39:17-18

When I was a little girl, our Sunday school teacher told us that everyone had two fathers: a daddy like mine and the Lord Jesus, a strong, invisible Father who watched over us from faraway heaven. For years afterward, I imagined a vast divide between heaven and Earth. Then an unexpected event proved that the Lord in His heaven is closer than I ever thought.

I was working at a bank as head teller. We arrived an hour before the bank opened each morning to process the typical avalanche of night deposits. Because most were stuffed with cash, we rushed to finish all transactions and stow excess money in the main vault before unlocking the front doors.

That day, I was running behind schedule. At 9:00 A.M., the first customer walked into the lobby. I heard the other tellers chatting with her. I was out of sight in the drive-through area, hurriedly strapping cash for the vault. Then it got eerily quiet.

With my arms full of money, I spun around to see what was going on, and nearly slammed into a tall man in a hooded ski jacket and face mask, waving a nine-millimeter handgun. He ordered me to lie facedown on the floor and screamed at one of my co-workers to collect the huge amount of cash I'd dropped. Then I felt cold metal against my right temple.

"DO IT NOW OR I'LL KILL HER!" he roared.

Faces of precious loved ones flew through my mind. I didn't want to leave them. Not like this.

"Oh, Father, please help us," I silently prayed, my heart thundering in my chest.

Suddenly, a firm but gentle hand rested against my left shoulder. It was soothing, unlike the frantic, trembling hand pressing a gun to my head.

"Be still. He's leaving soon. It will be all right."

My spirit relaxed when I heard my Heavenly Father's voice, calm in the midst of chaos.

A few moments later, the robber had what he came for and darted out the door. No one was hurt. Rattled, yes, but we survived the ordeal in one piece. Just as the Lord said we would.

Later, I realized that if it were not for the scariest four minutes of my life, I might never have accepted what many Christians know to be true. When we're alone, we're not by ourselves. No matter what, our Heavenly Father is always with us.

The bank robber got away with a bag of cash. What I received in return was far more precious—irrefutable proof of our Father's love.

My Prayer

*Father, thank you for your constant presence
in our lives. Because of your love, we are never
alone. For this and so much more, we praise
and honor you.*

Amen.

Never Alone

By Susan M. Heim

When my spirit grows faint within me, it is you who watch over my way.
~Psalm 142:3

Loneliness engulfed me as I waved goodbye to my parents. They had spent the past few days helping my children and I move into our apartment, but now they were heading back to their home, a two-hour drive away. I'd left my husband and the first house I'd ever owned to move into a small two-bedroom apartment with my sons, ages four and one. With my parents' departure, the frightening reality hit that I was solely responsible for these little boys and our survival.

My younger son was napping in his crib, and my other son headed out to the screened-in porch in the back of our second-floor apartment. He was excited to see all the ducks swimming in the small lake behind us, but all I could see was despair. I flung myself onto my bed and sobbed my heart out to God, praying for the courage to face the daunting future ahead of me.

After the tears had subsided somewhat, I heard my son speaking to someone. "My name is Dylan," I heard him say. "What's your name?" A female voice responded, and I realized that she must be walking on the ground below. I couldn't hear her response, but my son told her, "I just moved here with my mom and my brother. Where do you live?"

Their conversation continued for a short while, and then it grew quiet. I called Dylan into my bedroom to ask who he had been talking to. "It's a really nice lady, Mommy. She lives right below us, and she has a girl named Jenny who's the same age as me! She said that we can play together anytime."

In the years to come, we became good friends with Jenny and her single mom, Sherry. We took care of each other's children and cats, played with our kids at the park together, and shared the challenges of single parenting. One day, it hit me that God had not left me alone. He'd sent my friendly little boy out to the balcony to bring us some friends. And he'd given me the strength and courage I needed to provide a good life for my family.

My Prayer

Dear Father, you assure us that we are never alone. May I seek comfort in your words when I feel lonely or scared. I know that you will never desert me in my time of need and will give me strength to face any situation that arises.

Amen.

Twelve Steps to God

By Jamie Lee

I can do all this through him who gives me strength.
~Philippians 4:13

The relationship I have with my Creator today was born from a broken heart. I had grown up knowing about God, but I never really knew God until I was in my early thirties and eleven years into a destructive marriage.

I found myself married to an addict, and our lives had gone from love and kindness to anger and isolation. I was miserable, but I did not believe I could survive without this man in my life.

I began attending Al-Anon meetings, where we discussed the 12 Steps and the spiritual awakening they invite into our lives. At every meeting, I recited the prayer, but I had yet to feel it in my heart. Still, I believed that God would bring me out of the darkness.

I depended on God to carry me every second of the day. When I woke, before I even opened my eyes, I welcomed God into my life: "Good morning, God. Please help me get out of bed; please help me get dressed; please help me make it through the day." I was living in the moment, unable to face my future or feel joy.

I knew I was dying in this marriage, and I also knew that I had to make changes.

One lonely night, I found myself alone and drowning in despair.

I dropped to my knees and confessed, "God, if you want this marriage to end, you have to end it—I can't."

Two days later, God answered. I came home after work and found a note from my husband. The note was scribbled on a small piece of lined pink paper and read, "Went to work in Montana." There was no explanation, no "I love you," and no "I'll call."

As I stood in my kitchen reading the note, a warmth and peace came over me. I felt my worries and troubles fly away. I felt a love and clarity I had never experienced before, and there was no fear. I knew exactly what I needed to do. It was time to file for divorce.

God opened my heart, and I experienced the spiritual awakening I had heard others speak of so often. I knew at that moment that my marriage had been finished for a long time; I had just refused to let go out of fear. I also knew the time for fear was over.

Seventeen years have passed. There have been times when doubt and fear have come back to me, but God always reminds me of His presence, and the peace returns. I think back on that day, on that moment, and how blessed I am. I chuckle when I remember how I believed I couldn't live without my husband. But, in a way, I was right. I didn't survive without him; I thrived. I am living a life of joy and purpose, thanks to the grace of God.

My Prayer

God, fill me with your power today. Help me to trust you as you provide abundant grace and mercy in my life. Let everyone I meet feel your love, your light, and your presence.

Amen.

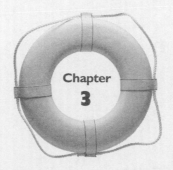

Chapter
3

Devotional Stories for Tough Times

Surrender to God

Jesus called out with a loud voice,
"Father, into your hands I commit my spirit."

~Luke 23:46

21

Bougainvilleas on the Bus Route

By Lindy Schneider

And the peace of God, which transcends all understanding, will guard your hearts and your minds in Christ Jesus. Finally, brothers and sisters, whatever is true, whatever is noble, whatever is right, whatever is pure, whatever is lovely, whatever is admirable — if anything is excellent or praiseworthy — think about such things.
~Philippians 4:7-8

"We can't leave Montana!" I told God. "My children need to stay where they have family and teammates and school friends." I frantically prayed that God would work out the details for us to stay, but He didn't. Despite business counseling, strategic plans, and our best efforts, our school supply store failed. And like a black hole, it seemed to suck away my life.

After a difficult search, my husband found work in Arizona. With aching hearts, we packed up our four children and everything we owned and moved. It was the worst time to move my daughter. She was beginning her senior year in high school and would have to leave all her friends behind and start at a new school. She sobbed into my shoulder, and I comforted her as best I could, but I didn't understand the "why" either.

Since I wanted to stay strong for my husband and kids, I thought it was better for me to journal than to voice my grievances. I began to compile a list of things we had lost. I wrote several pages and thought of more things to add every day:

We lost our beautiful home and moved into an apartment.

We moved away from the kids' beloved grandmother.

We gave up one car only to have the other one break down in the move.

The kids have no friends here.

As the list grew longer, I also committed to reading my Bible every day, but I could not find peace. I kept getting stuck on Philippians 4:8, which admonished me to think about things that are praiseworthy. In my pain, I argued with God. "If I could think of anything that was praiseworthy, I would think about that!"

One morning on my way to work, I was staring out the window of the city bus when I noticed a bush covered in flowers that were bright fuchsia. I asked a fellow commuter for the name of that bush, for I had never seen flowers that color before.

"Bougainvillea," she replied.

"Okay, God," I silently prayed, "I will thank you for the bougainvilleas."

From that moment, I began to see those bright pink flowers everywhere! I remembered my promise and thanked God each time I saw them. When I returned home to my apartment, there were bougainvillea petals strewn by the wind all across my path. It melted my heart to feel Him reaching out and saying, "Trust me."

We have been in Arizona for several years, and now I journal my blessings, not losses. My daughter and oldest son met their wonderful spouses here. My two younger sons have seen opportunities open to them that were never available in Montana. And every year, God brings those bougainvilleas to bloom, reminding me of how His constant love changed my heart, even when I couldn't see Him.

My Prayer

*Lord, I give you all those things that make
me anxious. I trust that you will work out all
the details of my family's needs, including our
financial needs. I pray that you will help me to
focus on your blessings — those things that are
praiseworthy — so that I might experience your
peace in the midst of my trials.*

Amen.

"You sent Moses a burning bush, God, but a bougainvillea works for me!"

Reprinted by permission of Stephanie Piro ©2011.

22

The Dance of Life

By Sandra Diane Stout

In the same way, the Spirit helps us in our weakness. We do not know what we ought to pray for, but the Spirit himself intercedes for us through wordless groans. And he who searches our hearts knows the mind of the Spirit, because the Spirit intercedes for God's people in accordance with the will of God.
~Romans 8:26-27

"Why me?" I walked out to the backyard, sat on the ground, and cried. I looked up toward the white clouds floating across the blue sky. "Why, God? Why did this have to happen?"

"Why not you?" He answered. "I know the plans I have for you."

After shedding a few tears, I realized that God does have a plan for my life, as He does for each of us. My husband, Gayle, had had a terrible farm accident and lost his right leg just below the knee. Even though it was part of a limb, I felt like I had lost the man I married. I knew he was still the same loving, caring, and hard-working person he always was, but I also knew life would be different.

After a time of grieving, I realized I had to let God lead me in the dance of life. Together, we began to flow with life's music. He gently nudged me in the back and lightly pushed me in one direction or another. I had to surrender willingly as He skillfully guided my footsteps. And as I danced with God, He led me through a tough season of my life.

During the first year of recuperation, my husband and I went to an agriculture meeting for handicapped farmers. There were several guys there with artificial limbs of various types. One young man in a wheelchair was paralyzed from the waist down. Another was paraplegic, caused by falling asleep at the wheel while driving his truck on the farm. He lay in the field for eighteen hours before anyone found him. Each man told his story.

Neither of us wanted to be there that day. But as Gayle and I listened to each personal story and observed the disabilities, God showed us that no matter what our circumstances, there are others who are dealing with more difficult handicaps. Each man was making the best of his situation, letting the disappointment in his life form a pearl of blessing, just as the oyster uses an irritating grain of sand to form a beautiful pearl. God taught us through the words of these men that our perspective makes all the difference.

My Prayer

Dear Heavenly Father, help me to trust you and to let you lead and guide me through the tough seasons of my life as well as the good times. Help me to surrender willingly to your guidance. May your blessings flow upon me this day as you lead me in the dance of life.

Amen.

Sweet Rest

By Mary Hughes

"Come to me, all you who are weary and burdened,
and I will give you rest."
~Matthew 11:28

In times of turmoil and great personal anguish, I used to find it difficult to sleep. In the deep of night, my mind would scramble from the very present troubles going on in my life to nightmarish visions of possible outcomes, the peace-stealing "what-ifs."

I remember a particular season of my life when the nighttime threatened to devour me. Our nineteen-year-old daughter had moved six-and-a-half hours away, determined to live her life the way she thought suitable. Her idea of suitable and ours were as distant as the miles between us. She wouldn't listen, and her father and I could not acquiesce. Our relationship with our daughter was on the verge of fracturing.

During the day, I battled despair by praying and keeping busy. In the silence of the night, however, I was bedeviled by negative, consuming thoughts. My mind became a battleground, a place where I waged war with my daughter's rebellion. Yet even in my imagination, I was unable to construct a happy ending.

Then, one day, I recognized that I had to quit trying to control the situation and completely release my daughter into God's hands. I finally came to terms with the fact that my struggle to control things was futile. Her father and I had done everything we could; we had said everything that could possibly be said, and none of it was working. I couldn't wage war with my daughter or with myself anymore. I opened the palms of my hands toward the sky and released my precious girl's life, her future, to God. It was then that my wrestling finally ceased.

I decided from then on that I would thank God for what He had in store for us and our daughter, regardless of the pain we were feeling or the outcome. And, oddly enough, in the midst of it all, I was able to see some of my own rebellion and ungodly attitudes. My eyes had been opened. Where I had once prayed for God to change my daughter, I began to pray for Him to change me instead.

It is by God's grace and His grace alone that our daughter found her way back. Because of His work in our lives, our relationship has not only been restored, but it is beautiful and authentic in a way it was not before. We know, however, that things do not always work out that way.

When trouble comes—and it has and will again—I remember the time I lifted my palms to God on behalf of my daughter, and I lift them up anew. I pray and ask God to guide and change my heart and attitudes where I err. I hand over my troubles and my feeble attempts to fix things. It is in this place of prayer that my burdens and troubles move from my open palms to the shoulders of a loving God more than capable of handling every situation.

And it is there I find sweet rest.

My Prayer

*Lord, when life's troubles come my way, I will
lift my eyes and my palms to you. I trust you
completely with my burdens and their outcomes.
In you, I find my rest.*

Amen.

Safe in the Arms of Jesus

By Michelle Stewart

He tends his flock like a shepherd: He gathers the lambs in his arms and
carries them close to his heart; he gently leads those that have young.
~Isaiah 40:11

We had just moved across the country with our three young children to pastor a church. The small congregation of about thirty people welcomed us with warmth and acceptance. Within a month, the church had doubled in size, but the "new" people and the "old" people were finding it difficult to adjust to one another. We worked hard at assimilating the two groups and prayed for unity.

At this time, we were excited about the pending arrival of our fourth child, and the church waited in anticipation with us! At twenty-seven weeks of pregnancy, I woke up not feeling well. I worked at home in the morning, but by noon I knew something wasn't right, so my husband drove me to the doctor. He told me I was in full labor and would be having a baby that day! I accepted the news with a heavy heart, aware of the risks, but prayed for a miracle.

I was taken by ambulance to the hospital, and our beautiful little girl was born less than an hour later, weighing only one pound, three ounces. She was a fighter and had the best possible medical care. The doctor came to me and asked if we wanted them to keep trying to keep her alive. I cried, frantically wondering how I could possibly answer that question! I asked him what he thought, and he said that he really didn't want to cause her more pain. I told him to do what was best for her. So after two hours of struggling for life on this Earth, my baby girl, Claire, went to heaven to rest in the arms of Jesus. Our hearts were broken. Our dreams for Claire had been shattered, and we cried out to God in our pain.

I remembered being in the delivery room—where I knew that the chances of Claire's survival were low—and hearing God tell me that this experience would be good for the church. It was not something I wanted God to be whispering in my ear at that point! I wanted Him to tell me that she would live and everything would be okay. But that's not what I heard.

When Claire died, everyone in the church rallied around us. They supported us, loved us, and grieved with us. More than 100 people attended her funeral. God took a difficult situation and used it to unify our church. He created a strong, solid bond between all of us, and the church grew in love. It was a love that extended outside the walls, and other people were drawn to it. The two groups in our church linked arms and hearts to become one body. The church grew to 1,200 in the ten years we were there.

The ache in our hearts is still there and always will be, but we know that Claire is cradled in the arms of Jesus. I look forward to the day when I will hold her again. The little seed of her life was planted in the ground, and from it grew a strong, full tree—a church with branches that extend far, offering shade and comfort to those who need it.

My Prayer

*Thank you, Father, that you are our shepherd
who leads us and cares for us. Help us to trust
you as we grow in our faith. We acknowledge that
it is your amazing love that brings us together in
unity now and forever.*

Amen.

Being Thankful

By Marilyn Turk

… give thanks in all circumstances;
for this is God's will for you in Christ Jesus.
~1 Thessalonians 5:18

"I'm sorry, but we've decided to give the position to another candidate." Those too-familiar words echoed through my mind as I set down the phone.

Another door closed. It had been more than a year since my company merged and I was laid off. At first, I was confident that twenty-five years of experience with the same employer would land me another job easily. However, the months dragged on, and the severance pay and the unemployment compensation ran out, forcing me to withdraw from my 401(k) to pay bills. I applied for every position available in my field. Still, no job offer. Every glimmer of hope dissolved into tears of disappointment. Daily, I appealed to God, asking for guidance and searching the Bible for answers. I desperately tried to hold onto hope and trust God to take care of me, but the future looked bleak. My prayers seemed to be unheard. At the age of fifty, I was no longer a desirable candidate, since a younger person could be trained for half my former income. I felt as if God had written me off like everyone else, and I was no longer necessary to society, other than my creditors.

A friend asked me if I would consider moving because, as an empty-nester, I didn't need a big house. I was willing to make sacrifices, but giving up my house was not one of them. My home was my last bastion of security, an answer to prayer ten years before. I couldn't believe God would want me to move. This was the home where I would live in my old age, where my future grandchildren would visit.

One day, I came across the Bible verse, "... give thanks in all circumstances; for this is God's will for you in Christ Jesus" (1 Thessalonians 5:18). How could I do that? How could I be thankful for losing my job, running out of money, and possibly losing even more? To say I was thankful for these things would be hypocritical.

Then it occurred to me to thank God for what I had been given. I could thank God for my former career—the experience I had gained, the people I'd met and places I'd been. I thanked God for the home He had given me to raise my children and for the memories we had shared there. Then I realized God had given me the home when I needed it, and it had served its purpose. I had trusted Him with my past; therefore, I could trust Him with my future.

Being thankful allowed me to let go and opened my mind to other possibilities, even if it meant moving. Once I decided I was willing to move, I had three different job offers in other states. It's been more than six years since I moved. I love my new home, and God has blessed me beyond my expectations. I now know how to be thankful "in all circumstances."

My Prayer

Dear Lord, thank you for everything you've given me. Knowing I have you to lean on when I am feeling worried makes my decisions easier. Remind me to place my trust in you, and in everything give thanks.

Amen.

Don't Ask Me

By Kaye Kinsey

I have been crucified with Christ and I no longer live, but Christ lives in me.
The life I now live in the body, I live by faith in the Son of God,
who loved me and gave himself for me.
~Galatians 2:20

The first time I remember him molesting me was in my mama's house. I was about seven. It was on a Thursday, my mama's grocery day. He sent my brother and neighbor out to play. Then he locked the door....

Time passed. He moved. I grew up. I went to college, married, and had a daughter. Finally, as an adult, I told my family at different times what had happened. Daddy was sick. My brother was furious. However, my mother's reaction was anything but what I expected. With disgust in her voice, she bitterly stated, "I don't believe that. It never happened. You were never alone with him." Although I gave her details to prove that I wasn't lying, she still defended him... her brother.

I cried out, "If you ever deny what happened to me again, I will never come around you, and you will never see my daughter." From that day on, neither her brother, nor what he did to me, was mentioned in our conversations.

Mama, however, still continued a close relationship with him.

She took him out to eat and to his medical appointments, and visited him regularly.

Dementia has affected many of my mother's relatives, so it wasn't a shock when Mama began to show signs of it. Even in the early stages, she was not able to handle business affairs. It was that condition that led Mama to ask something of me that I didn't think I could do. She asked me to handle the funeral arrangements for her brother who had just died.

The thought of it made me sick. I had told other family members that I would never attend his funeral. Now my mother was asking me to contact a minister, get burial clothes, telephone family members, notify the insurance company, and open my home as a place for the family to gather.

How could she? I hated him. I hated what he'd done to me. I hated that she had chosen her love for him over her love for me.

I began to pray. "Lord, are you giving me an opportunity to forgive him? I don't want to. Are you giving me the opportunity to heal a wound that my mother caused? I don't want to, not this way. I can't do it."

But I knew the whole time that God wanted me to forgive. Still, on and on I prayed, reminding the Lord of all that had happened. He continued to speak to my heart.

At last, I recalled a verse I had claimed many times in my life—Philippians 4:13: "I can do all this through him who gives me strength."

Sitting behind Mama at a funeral I had planned, while a gentle rain fell on the tent above us, I found a peace that had eluded me for years. And it happened because God called me to do what I thought I couldn't do... truly forgive.

My Prayer

Lord, for your strength and wisdom, I praise you.
Even though I may struggle with forgiveness, my
life is in your hands. You never promised us an
easy path, but you did promise us salvation if we
keep our eyes upon you.

Amen.

In the Father's Hands

By Michele Cushatt

All your children will be taught by the LORD, and great will be their peace.
~Isaiah 54:13

When I first became a mother, the future bloomed with dreams to last a lifetime. I sang sweet songs as I rocked my little ones to sleep. I planned special family days and took enough pictures to fill dozens of albums. I read stories and prayed with each child before bed. In the beautiful simplicity of those early years, I didn't realize being a mother would include challenges and heartache along the way, especially during the teen years.

Our oldest son was sixteen years old when he decided not to come home. House rules proved too confining, too limiting to his preferred way of life. And so he decided to live with another family member, severing his relationship with us. The days and weeks in the wake of his departure moved agonizingly slow. Phone calls were ignored, and text messages went unacknowledged. Learning to set the dinner table with four plates instead of five brought me to tears. Tucking two children into bed instead of three left a devastating hole in my heart. Friends and family tried to reassure me with their own stories of teenage rebellion. After all, they'd matured and turned out okay—our son would, too. I tried to find hope in their encouragement, but the grief over my son's absence trumped all other emotions.

Weeks turned into months, and slowly our family adjusted to life without one of its members. We still planned fun family days, took pictures, and said prayers at bedtime, but with a dulled joy. Never was my third child far from my heart. Daily, I prayed—boy, did I pray!—that God would lead our prodigal son home, and that we, as his parents, would have the grace and forgiveness to embrace him if and when he did.

In the end, he was gone for nearly six months, a painful stretch of time that seemed much longer while in the middle of it. In hindsight, however, I now realize I learned a significant lesson through the waiting, something that has served me well as I continue my journey as a mother.

As much as I'd like to keep my children safely within my home where I can teach, protect and love them day in and day out, a day is coming when each will leave to build their own life. Ultimately, this is what we want, what we've been training them for—adulthood. Mistakes will be made, and sometimes I won't agree with the paths they choose. But this reassurance gives me peace: Our Heavenly Father has promised to faithfully lead my children on their life's journey, to the very end. Over time, my role will change, and I'll need to let go so they can live. But God's hands will hold them steady, and my children will never be far from home.

My Prayer

Father God, I am grateful that I can trust you
with the hearts and lives of my children.
When I feel like I am barely hanging on,
let your peace and tranquility fill my heart.
I find comfort in knowing that you are
a beloved shepherd, who will never let
one of your precious sheep become lost.

Amen.

A Wise and Loving Coach

By Ken Hornok

And our hope for you is firm, because we know that
just as you share in our sufferings, so also you share in our comfort.
~2 Corinthians 1:7

I called the head elder at my church and told him, "I don't know what to do. I can't study, let alone preach. I can't do any ministry right now. I don't know when I'll be able to come to the office again. What should I do?"

As the pastor, I thought I needed to be in control of every situation, but I was at my wit's end. A house fire ten months earlier left us living in a small rental unit, commuting our kids to their schools. We had insurance negotiations, decision overload, and the unpleasant task, at least for me, of shopping to replace the items we had lost. Also, I had contracted to do all the painting on our remodeled house, and that deadline loomed. In the meantime, we discovered my wife had cancer in her ear and head. Little did we know that our teenaged daughter would be blinded by meningitis one month after my wife's surgeries.

I had always heard that God doesn't give us more than we can bear. First Corinthians 10:13 says that God "will not let you be tempted beyond what you can bear." But does this verse apply to our sufferings, as well? It felt like God had overloaded me and my family at this time. Knowing that God is a wise and loving coach, not a hard taskmaster, I had to accept His training process. His rigorous discipline would develop my spiritual muscles, but wasn't He going too far?

When I read 2 Corinthians 1:8-9, it answered my question. Writing about the hardships he suffered in Asia, Paul said, "We were under great pressure, far beyond our ability to endure, so that we despaired of life itself." Yes, it is possible to have more than we can bear, but verse 9 gives the purpose for it: "But this happened that we might not rely on ourselves but on God." But I felt stranded by God, and that's when I called the elder and asked for help.

Graciously, the church leaders told me to take off as much time as I needed, and our associate pastor handled all church functions for the next three weeks. People ministered to us and our children in meaningful ways during the following months. I'm glad I asked for help.

Gradually, we found our footing again. We moved back into our house, my wife's cancer has not returned, and our daughter regained her vision after three months. Although I had felt like I could never be useful again, I learned the paradox that God can use my weaknesses more than my competencies.

My Prayer

*Father, help me not to be a "Lone Ranger
Christian." Although I rely on you, I also need
help from other Christians. May I be humble
enough to ask for it and receive it.*

Amen.

29

Minnie Moo

By Jennifer Quasha

*Trust in the LORD with all your heart and lean not
on your own understanding; in all your ways submit to him,
and he will make your paths straight.*
~Proverbs 3:5-6

I rescued Minnie from the back corner of a dirty, dark kennel, her temporary home. She had been driven north to New York from West Virginia by a rescue organization that uses foster families to house strays while they try to find them homes. When I first picked up her ten-pound frame, Minnie was catatonic from trauma. Fear pulsed thorough her body, but age and experience hadn't yet taught her to defend herself. She was so frightened that only her eyes moved, watching me with terror. I placed her in a cage in my car and went on with my day. My next stop: Bible study.

I pulled in at the same time as my friend, Serena. I stood waiting for her as she got out of her car. I asked her excitedly if she wanted to see my new foster dog, a shepherd-mix named Minnie, who was in the back of my car. Serena froze. She told me that she had just lost Hudson, their fourteen-year-old shepherd mix, two days before.

Serena explained that Hudson had passed away at the vet's office after a sudden illness. Shaken, Serena walked to the back of my car to see Minnie. In a whisper, she told me that she had adopted Hudson fourteen years earlier from a friend who was fostering her. Hudson turned out to be the best dog they had ever had. We looked at each other and knew that God was there.

After I brought Minnie home, if she wasn't resting in her cage, she was in my arms. She spent hours papoosed against my chest. I could feel her faint heartbeat, and I hoped that she could feel mine, trying to beat love and a sense of peace back into her. Once in a while, I would stop in front of a mirror to look at her little head peeking out of the top of my sweatshirt. The love I felt for her was so pure. Loving her brought out the very best in me. Hour by hour, day by day, I loved her more. Regular food and love had begun the process of healing. She was alert and curious, and her eyes had softened. The puppy within her was starting to blossom. Serena brought her husband to meet her, and the process of moving Minnie to her forever home—and away from me—was happening fast.

God's hand at work was clearer than a glass of water, but my heart was breaking. I knew that Minnie had found the best home possible, and that I would be able to see her if I wanted to, but letting her go was testing my once-generous heart. I knew that I needed to follow the path that He laid before me, but my soul ached with the loss. When Serena came to pick up Minnie and led her away on her brand-new leash, I knew, however painful and hard, that I was doing what God wanted me to do.

Now, having fostered more dogs and finally adopting Sugar—a beagle that is truly right for our family—I am reminded that God's plan is always right. We may not see it, but if we ask for His help and follow Him, He will never lead us astray.

My Prayer

Heavenly Father, thank you for the many gifts
you continue to give to me. I know that
I feel closer to you when I do what you have
called me to do, but please give me the strength to
follow your will, today and always.
In Jesus Christ's name, I pray.

Amen.

Chapter
4

Devotional Stories for Tough Times

Power of Prayer

"In my distress I called to the LORD; I called out to my God. From his temple he heard my voice; my cry came to his ears."

~2 Samuel 22:7

The Other Side of the Curtain

By Jennifer McDonald

Carry each other's burdens, and in this way you will fulfill the law of Christ.
~Galatians 6:2

I lay in the hospital bed that first night after surgery, my thoughts clouded by medication and intense pain. I could hear the patient on the other side of the curtain moaning, and worse... retching. She was obviously as miserable as I was. It was an unlucky period in my life. This was my third surgery in four months' time. Added to that, we were a military family, stationed far from our home state, though blessed to have a caring church and community.

Earlier in the day, after my roommate and I had each been wheeled in from the recovery room, our respective families had visited. Her visitors had been loud, to my irritation. Her two young children had screamed as their grandmother prodded them to say their goodbyes and head home. I gathered from the inadvertently overheard conversation that the woman on the other side of the curtain was going through a divorce. Still, I doubt that compassion was my first response as I lay wracked with pain, attempting to rest in spite of the discomfort and nausea.

She got sick again. Domino effect—I got sick again. I pushed

The Other Side of the Curtain : Power of Prayer   111

the call bell for the nurse, hoping for some relief. Nurses came in to both of us, quietly soothed and administered medications, and then left us to rest. The curtain stayed drawn between us; we had not seen each other once. Yet, as I lay there, miserable, I became aware that another human being lay feet away from me. She was suffering, too... but suffering more than physically. Compassion overwhelmed me, and I felt God prodding me to look beyond myself for a moment. Somehow, in the dark, with nothing to lose, boldness came over me.

"I don't know what your beliefs are... but I just want you to know... I'm praying for you right now," I whispered.

Silence. Then... quiet crying, and a quavering whisper back. "Thank you."

"What is your name?"

"Julie."

And that was all.

We never exchanged more words, but as I awoke through the night, I was no longer as conscious of my own pain as I was of hers. And each time I awoke, I lifted a heartfelt prayer for Julie's recovery and for the situation she would be facing when she went home.

She was discharged the next day with very few words between us. It was several more days before I was released. Still, years later, whenever I remember Julie, I say a prayer for her.

My Prayer

Dear Lord, please remind me to look past my own
pain and see the need in other people's lives.
Let me not become so hardened by my own
problems that I forget to be compassionate and
reach out in your name.

Amen.

31

Partners in Prayer

By Tammy A. Nischan

The LORD is my shepherd, I lack nothing.
He makes me lie down in green pastures,
he leads me beside quiet waters,
he refreshes my soul.
He guides me along the right paths for his name's sake.
~Psalm 23:1-3

Attending a writer's conference just seven months after losing my teenage son to cancer was the last thing I really wanted to do. However, I knew that at some time I had to make the choice to step back out into the world. Since writing had become a healing way for me to deal with my grief, many of my friends had encouraged me to see what God could teach me through this conference.

As I took my seat in a workshop on prayer (something I needed greatly), someone who knew of my son's illness asked me to come meet another mom whose son was fighting leukemia. Unknowingly, this lady asked, "How is your son doing?" I began to cry as I shared that Nick had passed away. We hugged, and I returned to my seat.

A lady I had never met had taken the seat next to mine. I leaned over and asked if she possibly had a tissue. As she reached into her purse, she realized I was crying. She took my hand and began sweetly introducing herself. She had only said a few words when I heard her mention that she and her husband were planning a marriage retreat in the near future. Tears filled my eyes again as I realized that my marriage had become strained, difficult, and painful due to grief. I briefly shared Nick's story with her before the session began. As the workshop ended, the speaker encouraged us to come forward if we needed a prayer partner. My new friend, Carolyn, turned to me and asked if I would like to be her prayer partner.

We left the workshop and walked to the prayer room where Carolyn prayed over me and my marriage. A few months later, I found myself traveling several hundred miles from my home along with my husband to attend the marriage retreat Carolyn had told me about. Not only had she invited us to come, but she had paid for every expense of the trip for us as a gift. At the retreat, my husband and I renewed our vows and developed several new friendships.

Grief almost kept me from attending a writing conference. Thankfully, God gave me the strength to attend and, in doing so, allowed me to meet my lifelong friend and prayer partner. On top of that, God blessed my marriage with an opportunity for refreshment and renewal.

My Prayer

Dear Lord, thank you for promising to walk with us even through the valley of the shadow of death. Lord, because of you, we can walk this dark road without fear of evil. You promise to comfort and guide us, and, best of all, you promise to restore our souls! Thank you, Father, for being our shepherd. Thank you for guiding us in paths of righteousness for your name's sake. Help us trust you as we walk in your will.

Amen.

32

Exchanged Gifts

By Denise A. Dewald

Rejoice with those who rejoice; mourn with those who mourn.
~Romans 12:15

I walked into the surgery waiting room with my devotional booklet in hand, fully intending to read it. But as I sat down and looked at the pages, it was hard to concentrate on anything but my husband. Though his particular surgery wasn't life-threatening, it demanded my full attention. I shifted my position and tried once more to read, but found myself being drawn to the conversation of a group of people to my right.

"The doctor should be calling us soon. She's been in surgery for a long time."

"Yes, but he told us the tumor was big."

"Let's join hands and pray."

I listened as this small group of people openly asked God for healing and strength. I glanced around the room and noticed uncomfortable looks, shuffling feet, and stares. I marveled at the courage of these Christians to publicly proclaim their faith without a thought for what others might think. I wanted to get up and add my own hands to their circle of prayer, but I held back. As usual, I was worried about what people would think of me. Instead, I silently joined in their prayer.

I learned they were friends and relatives of a young woman undergoing brain surgery. She was also a wife and mother of a small baby.

I listened carefully as they spoke of Christ and His power in their lives. Optimistic words of encouragement were exchanged, and they strengthened one another with discussions of family and church life. One man, a schoolteacher, offered humorous stories of classroom antics. The laughter these stories brought prompted me to ask myself if I could be so relaxed in a similar situation. They simply left everything in God's hands.

Finally, the call they'd been waiting for came. I watched intently as the young husband of the woman in surgery walked purposefully to the phone. The waiting friends and relatives were all standing. Their faces showed no worry, and there was no nervous hand-wringing. There was only the calm, hopeful demeanor of those trusting in God's will, whatever that might be.

When the young man hung up the phone, he wasn't smiling. Looking at each of them, he quietly said, "They got most of it, but couldn't get it all."

The mother of the young woman fell back into her chair and began softly crying. I could no longer sit silently. I rose, my own tears now falling, and walked over to this dear woman. I put my arms around her and held her.

The thought that I might be intruding crossed my mind. But her need to share her pain was evident in the way she immediately buried her face in my shoulder. I knew my feelings of apprehension were unfounded. We sat there with the eyes of the entire room on us, crying together.

After a few minutes, she wiped her eyes and looked at me. With mild surprise in her voice, she said, "It's so unusual for a total stranger to come up to someone like this."

As we sat and talked, I was glad I had decided to share their suffering instead of sitting passively. Not only was I able to show them I cared, but through their strong example, I was encouraged to be more open in my own faith: we helped each other.

My Prayer

*Dear Lord, you know the situations and pain
that all your beloved children are going through.
Help us to reach out in love to others in their
time of need. Use us to comfort them and
lighten their burdens.*

Amen.

Making a Difference

By Ann Summerville

Until now you have not asked for anything in my name.
Ask and you will receive, and your joy will be complete.
~John 16:24

"I don't know why you keep going there," my husband shouted at me. "You don't have any qualifications to be counseling someone. You don't..."

The tirade continued along with him pointing his index finger at me and starting each sentence with "you."

He may have been right. I'd started volunteering at a local crisis pregnancy center one afternoon a week, filing and doing whatever office work they needed. With the lack of women volunteers to talk to the young girls, I agreed to take a training course and eventually met with each of the girls who came to the center to help them make a decision for their unplanned pregnancy. Most of the time, I cried more than they did. But if they agreed to give me their address, I followed up with periodic encouraging notes, letters, and cards.

His anger had begun at a fundraising banquet when the volunteers were recognized, and I stood along with many others who kept the crisis pregnancy center going. There was only one person in our family who should be in the spotlight and, according to him, it shouldn't be me.

That month had been heart-wrenching. One young lady was adamant that her parents would not welcome a mixed-race baby, and she had planned an abortion without their knowledge. Another lady whose child had recently drowned in a backyard sewer said, without a tear in her eye, that she wanted another baby to replace him.

While watching the finger-pointing of the red-faced man before me, I silently prayed. Was this where God wanted me to be? Was I making a difference?

I blocked out the noise and was overcome with peace, which was interrupted by the sharp tone of the telephone. As if on cue, the director of the center spoke softly into the phone. "I have someone here who wants to talk to you," she said in her kindly voice.

It was a young girl who had visited the center. Upon finding out that she was pregnant, she declared she could not have the baby. We cried and prayed together. Her boyfriend had joined the army and was leaving for boot camp. She was alone. The desperation in her voice was evident. I offered other alternatives, but she could not see anything but an abortion solving this "problem."

I held the phone close to my ear as I listened and heard a baby gurgle in the background.

"Your cards and letters helped me through," she said. "My boyfriend and I were married, and we have a beautiful baby girl. I wanted to thank you. I am so happy."

And she was—I could hear it in her voice. I have never seen that girl again, nor met her baby or husband, but as the front door slammed and rattled the house, my heart was at peace. I know I made a difference.

My Prayer

*Father in Heaven, I pray that in times of trouble,
we remember to look up to you first. Keep our
faith strong as we allow your mighty hand to
work in our lives and answer our prayers.*

Amen.

34

Carried Home

By Melanie Marks

*Take my yoke upon you and learn from me, for I am gentle and humble in
heart, and you will find rest for your souls.*
~Matthew 11:29

I didn't say anything, nothing. I just stayed balled up in my
sleeping bag, unable to force myself up. Just the thought of
moving made me cringe.

"Rise and shine!" our guide, Beth, chirped into our tent for the
third time.

Everyone around me groaned.

Today was the last day of our "Survival Course." If I made it
through today, I would get full credit. But I was sick. So sick. My feet
were sore, my back was sore, my whole, entire body was sore. I literally ached all over. Some of my pain was caused by the three weeks
of hiking and camping out in the freezing elements. But most of my
pain was simply because I was sick. Achingly, disastrously sick.

Finally, I dragged myself out of my sleeping bag, literally wob-
bling as I tried to stand. What was I going to do? I could barely
walk, yet we would be hiking all day. All day! My bones ached.
They felt brittle, like they would crumble into pieces at any minute.
And it wasn't just the agonizing pain or the freezing cold—there

was my backpack, too. It was heavy beyond belief. So heavy! It was backbreaking, even on the best of days. Today, I could barely lift it.

Still, painfully, I slouched into it, trembling from the weight.

What else could I do? There was certainly no turning back, as we had been hiking for over three weeks. There was no staying here, either, since the camp was already disassembled. We were out in the middle of nowhere. It was hopeless. Although I knew I was headed for tragedy, I started to hike.

My heart plummeted when the snow began to fall and kept falling. Finally, I had to stop. I couldn't go on, not another step. Through my tears, I started praying to my Heavenly Father. I asked Him to help me, to somehow get me through this and safely home.

Slowly, I started to walk again, still praying as I trudged along.

But soon—it was so strange—I noticed my backpack felt lighter. And then I couldn't even feel it! I really couldn't, not at all. I kept checking to see if it was even on my back. And then I noticed something else: I couldn't feel my body. All the terrible aches and pains were gone.

It was astounding. Truly.

My Heavenly Father had heard my prayers. No, I wasn't brought into a nice, warm, toasty cabin. But in my hour of need, He had lightened my load. My burdens had been lifted. My Father carried me home.

My Prayer

*Heavenly Father, in our hour of need, you hear
our cries of pain and come to lighten our load.
Our burdens are lifted, and we are reminded that
you are ever present in these trying moments.*

Amen.

35

Chicken Soup for the Soul.

God Has a Sense of Humor

By Charles Lee Owens

... he who appoints the sun to shine by day, who decrees the moon and stars to shine by night, who stirs up the sea so that its waves roar — the LORD Almighty is his name.
~Jeremiah 31:35

God does have a sense of humor. Plain and simple, He enjoys a good laugh. Look around you and see the humor in our lives. Then think back to that one time when all hope was lost, when you were down to your last dollar, or you saw no way out. Then suddenly, unexpectedly, things were resolved. The resolution may not have been the direct answer to your question, but it was a way to close one door and open a new one.

There was a time when I was in college that I thought I would fail physics. Maybe "fail" is too strong a word, but I did not want to make anything less than an A in college. I was driven to achieve a certain GPA, but this physics class was on the verge of giving me not only a C, but potentially a D. I was devastated to say the least.

In my despair, I went to Sunset Cliffs one evening to complain to God. I took up my position along the cliffs about twenty feet up from the beach and stood there watching the sun set over a rather peaceful ocean. And then I began to complain bitterly about my lack of understanding and why God was not allowing me to achieve an A in physics.

It was then that God answered me... Distinctly, I heard His words to me, "It is going to be all right. Stop complaining." Then suddenly, out of a calm sea, a wave splashed up on the side of the cliff and drenched me! I looked around, and I was the only one there! And I laughed and laughed... God has a sense of humor after all. You know, I never did get that A, but I did pass the class without issue and never looked back.

To all of you who strain to believe, God is there. He listens. And when we are complaining about nothing, He might even show you His sense of humor!

My Prayer

Father, I place my worries and fears into your
mighty hands today. Lead me on the right path
and let me plainly see what to do. I thank you for
the joy you put into each day.

Amen.

Reprinted by permission of
Stephanie Piro ©2011.

A Conversation with God

By Madeleine M. Kuderick

But when you pray, go into your room, close the door
and pray to your Father, who is unseen. Then your Father,
who sees what is done in secret, will reward you.
~Matthew 6:6

W hen my son Ben was eight years old, I faced a difficult dilemma. Ben couldn't pass the standardized achievement test due to his dyslexia. So, according to state guidelines, he would have to be "retained" in third grade. Ben's self-esteem was already low, and I worried that "flunking" third grade might damage his fragile ego. Still, my only alternative was transferring him to a private school and pulling him away from the only school he'd known.

Every Sunday, I filed into church and dutifully recited memorized prayers, hoping to receive some divine wisdom. But, week after week, the school dilemma remained.

Then, one day, Ben bounced down the stairs and joined me in the kitchen.

"Guess what?" he said. "I know where you can hear God."

I set down the dishes and smiled at him. "Really?" I asked. "Where is that?"

I expected Ben to say he heard God in church or during catechism class where he was learning the Lord's Prayer. Instead, Ben put his hand to his heart.

"You hear him right here, Mommy," he said, looking down at his chest.

Ben's answer took my breath away.

"You're right!" I replied, feeling a warm blush cross my cheeks. "And what did God say to you?"

"Well, I built my Lego fort first," Ben began. "Then I lined up my Lego people..." He gazed off into the distance, remembering the hundreds of intricate blocks he'd assembled and the figurines he'd placed so perfectly. "Then I just decided to ask Him. 'So, God, how do you like my set-up?'"

I smiled, trying to imagine how God might've answered that question. Did He praise Ben's hard work or command him to obey his parents and clean up his messy room? But the answer was much simpler than that.

"God said I needed more red men," Ben explained.

Ben thought about it for a moment, and then he bolted upstairs where he and God spent the afternoon hunting underneath the bed for more red men.

Ben had a way of doing that — of reminding me about things I should've already known. In the weeks that followed, I began having my own conversations with God. Nothing formal or rehearsed. Just conversations. Questions about what to do next. In time, I began to hear answers in my own heart.

The next year, we transferred Ben to a private school for students with learning differences. His reading skills steadily improved, and his self-esteem grew. He began winning reading awards and speech contests and nabbing lead parts in the school plays. Over time, it became clear that transferring schools had been the absolute right decision.

Ben will be starting high school next year, and again I find myself facing a difficult school selection. But this time, I know just what to do. I think I'll have another conversation with God. I bet He can point me to a good high school with a few red men.

My Prayer

*Thank you for hearing our prayers, no matter
how great or small they may seem. Thank you for
caring about our problems and helping us to find
solutions that bring us a sense of peace.*

Amen.

Dollars from Heaven

By Sheri Palivoda

Looking at his disciples, he said: "Blessed are you who are poor, for yours is the kingdom of God. Blessed are you who hunger now, for you will be satisfied. Blessed are you who weep now, for you will laugh."
~Luke 6:20-21

t was one of the most difficult times of my life. I had graduated from college six months earlier and was unable to find a full-time job. I was living in my first apartment, which was sparsely furnished with a worn sofa, unstable coffee table, and two old lamps left behind by a previous tenant. I was working three part-time jobs and barely making ends meet. It was at this time in my life that I decided to return to church. I had been an avid churchgoer as a child, but had lost interest in my teens and early twenties. When Sunday came along, I didn't have much, but I managed to scrape up a dollar for the collection plate each week. During one mass, the lector read from Luke 6:20-21: "'Blessed are you who are poor, for yours is the kingdom of God. Blessed are you who hunger now, for you shall be satisfied. Blessed are you who weep now, for you will laugh.'" For some reason, this quote gave me hope, and I began to pray to God for help.

During the following weeks, my situation became more desperate. I was still having difficulty finding full-time employment, and my meager funds were depleting quickly. I didn't know how I was going to survive, but I continued to pray. Soon afterward, I began finding various amounts of money around the city where I lived. It seemed that everywhere I went—in parks, on busy street corners, and in front of stores—I would find at least a five- or ten-dollar bill lying on the ground. One night while I was cleaning up in a restaurant where I worked, I found four twenty-dollar bills lying on the floor. No one ever claimed them. Another evening, a stranger came into the bar, ordered one drink, finished it quickly, and left. He left me a generous tip—a fifty-dollar bill underneath a one-dollar bill. I never saw the man again.

This mystery money continued to materialize until I finally found steady work that was sufficient to support myself. The money stopped appearing as quickly as it started, and I haven't found money since.

I truly believe that this mysterious money was a gift from God. He knew that I was suffering, and He sent me this money when I really needed it. After relating this story to a colleague, she gave me a copy of this prayer, which hangs on my refrigerator to this day:

"My Lord God, I have no idea where I am going... I will trust you always though I may seem to be lost and in the shadow of death. I will not fear, for you are ever with me, and you will never leave me to face my perils alone."

Through my months of struggle, I learned that God is watching, and He is always there to help when you need Him. All you have to do is ask.

My Prayer

Lord, it is when we are desperate that we need to feel your presence most. Thank you for showering your gifts of love upon us. You are truly an awesome God.

Amen.

Hope for the Dying

By B. Lee White

Acknowledge and take to heart this day that the LORD is God in heaven above and on the earth below. There is no other.
~Deuteronomy 4:39

Working on a palliative/hospice ward takes a special kind of person. You deal with death on a daily basis. You take great care of these patients because they're dying and in pain. You get attached to them and their families, and then they die. It's this never-ending feeling of being glad they're not in pain anymore, but missing them.

I always felt bad for the patients whose family members dropped them off at the hospital, never to be seen again. If I had free time or needed to chart on my patients, I would sit with these patients so they wouldn't die alone. One of those forgotten patients was Mr. Smith. One Saturday, during report on the patients, it was commented that Mr. Smith was still alive. He had been unresponsive for two weeks, but for one exception: He kept reaching his arms above him and saying, "Help me, help me."

Usually, cancer patients would become unresponsive and then die about a week later. For a patient to hold on for two weeks was unnatural. His words had me worried that he was too scared to die.

As soon as I had the chance, I went into Mr. Smith's room and sat down in a chair next to him. I held his hand and started talking to him. I explained to him what heaven was like, with no pain or sorrow. I shared with him about Jesus and how to be saved. I told him I would pray for him to accept Jesus as his Lord and Savior, and that if he agreed he would be saved and go to heaven. I said he didn't have to repeat what I said out loud, but that Jesus would hear him if he said it in his heart. I prayed out loud for him and continued to hold his hand for about twenty minutes before I had to get back to work.

About fifteen minutes later, the charge nurse approached me and said that Mr. Smith had died. Tears filled my eyes, and joy filled my heart. I really felt that this man had been afraid to die because he didn't know what would happen to him. Once I explained to him the beauty on the other side, he had enough peace to make his final journey.

My Prayer

Dear Lord, use me to find those who are far from you and haven't heard about your wonderful kingdom. Please spark the flame in me to share the Holy Spirit with others who need it most. In your glorious name...

Amen.

Chicken Soup for the Soul

The Gift of Time

By Rhonda Hensley

There is a time for everything,
and a season for every activity under the heavens.
~Ecclesiastes 3:1

"It might be time," my son-in-law nervously announced before I could barely get the word "hello" out. Our daughter, Amy, was experiencing labor pains. The doctor was attempting to stop them because she wasn't quite near enough to her due date to let nature take its course.

We began preparations immediately to depart on the four-and-a-half-hour trek just in case the situation merited our presence. We had been there for the birth of our other grandchildren and were determined to make every effort to be there for the arrival of our newest addition. Brent phoned us a few hours later to inform us they still had not been successful in stopping Amy's labor, and he felt sure she was going to have the baby.

After three attempts at stopping the process, our granddaughter, Addyson, made her debut into the world three and a half weeks shy of her expected arrival date. Obviously, she had her mother's tenacity and was determined she would come on her own timetable. With camera and two other children in tow, we patiently sat in the waiting area anticipating our first glimpse of the new addition.

A nurse finally made her way to the waiting area to present the news that Addyson had arrived; however, we would not be able to see her because she had been taken to the NICU. We would be able to see Amy as soon as they had her ready.

It is not unusual for premature babies to be taken to the NICU, so I really didn't become too alarmed by the news. I just thought it was more for precautionary measures than any other reason. Unfortunately, these assumptions proved to be far from the truth.

Addyson was in serious condition and needed to be transported to another facility more equipped for her condition. It wasn't until the next morning when her parents met with the doctors that we learned how short her time on Earth was expected to be. "Maybe a few days at the most," the doctors expressed. We were informed she had been born with a very rare genetic kidney disease. The disease causes the kidneys to be so enlarged that they impede the development of the lungs.

We knew that only God could determine Addyson's time on Earth. We requested prayer from many sources. People all over our country and other countries heard about this precious little girl and were diligently lifting her up in prayer. Thousands of people logged onto her web page regularly to check on her progress and encourage her parents through messages.

Addyson surpassed the medical community's expectations. She lived for more than eight weeks, providing an opportunity for her parents to show her their love and spend precious time with her.

God had a season for Addyson, and even though her time on Earth was brief, we know she fulfilled her purpose: to bring thousands before the throne of our Heavenly Father. In this, we find comfort.

My Prayer

Lord, I ask you to comfort those who mourn the loss of a child or a grandchild. Please heal their broken hearts and provide them with the strength to go on in life without their loved one.

Amen.

Never Beyond His Reach

By Kathleen Kohler

"For the Son of Man came to seek and to save the lost."
~Luke 19:10

When our son, Joe, spiraled into the world of drugs and gangs at age sixteen, I wondered, "Where is God?" Countless times, I fell to my knees broken-hearted, tears streaming down my face. I pleaded, "Lord, please watch over Joe, our precious lost lamb. Protect him and keep him safe. Lord, show him the way home."

Joe's choices plunged him into a frightening culture beyond our ability to reach him. Nothing we did could pull him back, but he never escaped God's watchful eye. Powerless, we watched as drugs and gangs choked out everything decent in Joe's life.

For six years, Joe wandered in and out of our lives, and away from the love and safety of our home. We continued to love him, and daily we prayed together and waited for him to emerge from the fog he was in. The turning point came one night when his dangerous lifestyle cornered him in a dark alley.

A rival gang member stood behind him, a revolver gripped in his hand, finger poised on the trigger. With a gun barrel jammed against the back of his head, Joe braced himself for the bullet. Penned in by buildings on both sides, there was no escape. He closed his eyes and waited for the shot.

Without warning, the gang member's arm went limp and fell to his side, still clutching the gun. After several futile attempts to lift his arm, he said, "Get out of here."

Paralyzed by fear, Joe hesitated.

"Go on. Get out of here," the voice yelled into the darkness.

Joe didn't look back. He raced forward, half-stumbling as he ran from the alley. Standing on a dark city street, his clothes soaked from sweat and drizzling rain, Joe realized the path he'd been racing down had nearly cost him his life. He'd been spared certain death, not by a rival gang member, but by Someone greater.

For years, we watched as God, compelled by His immeasurable love and mercy, pursued our son. The Lord followed him to crack houses, parties, gang activities, and behind jail walls. More than once during those years, we saw evidence of God's protective hand on Joe's life. Each new circumstance brought waves of fear, panic, and grief. Soon, we realized the Lord controlled the outcome of every situation. We gained comfort and an underlying peace in the midst of the turmoil.

God knocked loud on Joe's heart that night in the alley. It changed his perspective and the direction of his life.

Although his journey led us down a path of anguish and heartache, there we encountered the God who pursues. His relentless love has the power to follow our wayward children, no matter where they go—even to dangerous places. Because I know God reached into an alley in the dark of night and spared our son, I worry less and trust Him more with life's daily events.

My Prayer

Thank you, Lord, that you know exactly
where my child is. Help me trust you in every
circumstance and have the peace that comes from
knowing you're in control.

Amen.

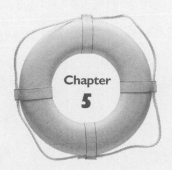

Chapter
5

Devotional Stories for Tough Times

Divine Signs

"'… This will be a sign between me and you for the generations to come, so you may know that I am the LORD, who makes you holy.'"

~Exodus 31:13

41

Ladybug Love

By Melissa Wootan

"I have set my rainbow in the clouds,
and it will be the sign of the covenant between me and the earth."
~Genesis 9:13

wasn't feeling very cheerful as I walked down the store aisles overflowing with Christmas decor. This Christmas season would mark the second anniversary of my daughter's death on December 18, 2008. She was buried on her seventeenth birthday, December 23. No, I wasn't feeling much holiday cheer at all.

Where was God in all of this? My heart ached so. I missed my daughter, my Kyley-Bug, as we called her.

"How are you?" I recognized the lady speaking to me. She went to church with my mother-in-law.

"Well, honestly, I'm not doing that great," I answered her as I proceeded to tell her all about Kyley's anniversary date coming up and exactly how I felt about that. Yeah, I figured she would run for the hills as soon as I was finished, but instead she put her arm around me and asked what she should pray for.

"Is there anything that is special to you, that reminds you of her—something that you would recognize as a sign that she's okay?"

"Ummmm... " I stuttered. I hadn't expected that from her. I couldn't think. Oh, of course, ladybugs! "Well, we get really excited over ladybugs now because of her nickname. It just reminds us of her."

"Well, then, I will pray for an infestation of ladybugs for you. Ladybugs everywhere." She hugged me goodbye, and we both went on our way.

Over the next week, I kept an eye open. Come on, ladybugs! Where are you? I could really use a sign. Thanksgiving was in a few days, a time for thanks and family, and I was finding it difficult to be thankful when my heart was so broken.

"God, haven't you heard the prayers? Where are the ladybugs? It's just that it would do so much for our souls."

Nothing, no ladybugs. Thanksgiving arrived, and as we prepared to gather at my sister's, my son walked out the front door ahead of us. My husband and I followed.

"Mom! A ladybug! It's a sign!" We rushed over to see his ladybug. "Dad, you have ladybugs all over you!" I looked at my husband. My son was right. They were everywhere. Tons of them. We laughed and brushed them away so that we could get into the car. As we sat in the car preparing to leave, we looked up at the house and saw hundreds of ladybugs blanketing our home.

God hadn't left unanswered prayers nor did He deny me the sign that refreshed my spirit and reminded me of what a loving father He is. He simply saved the answer for a day when He knew it would mean the most.

My Prayer

*Oh, great Heavenly Father, you know the needs
and hearts of every one of your children.
Thank you for being faithful, even when my spirit
is faint. It is you who sustains me
when I need it most.*

Amen.

"This Thanksgiving, we give thanks for family, turkey... and ladybugs!"

Reprinted by permission of
Stephanie Piro ©2011.

42

Chicken Soup for the Soul

Consider the Daisies

By Janeen Lewis

"If that is how God clothes the grass of the field, which is here today and tomorrow is thrown into the fire, will he not much more clothe you— you of little faith?"
~Matthew 6:30

"**W**e'll be okay, honey," my brightest voice mustered. In reality, my heart was heavy.

My husband, Jesse, a state government worker, called to break the news of a proposal for twelve unpaid furlough days for the next year. We had already endured the effects of six furlough days.

Jesse and I had become a one-income family in 2006 so that I could care for our newborn son, Andrew. Our nation's economic meltdown followed our decision. Grocery expenses rose, and gas prices skyrocketed while we lived on a less-than-average income. But we were thrifty and continually hopeful, and we had another child, our daughter, Gracie. For four years, God's provisions amazed me. Now, as we anticipated lost income, doubt chipped away at my faith.

At the same time, a drought plagued us. Though I watered faithfully, my petunias and Gerber daisies sagged like my forlorn spirit. After weeks, the rain came. Since summer had slipped into autumn, the downpour seemed inconsequential.

"Let's go for a walk, Mama!" Andrew exclaimed the next day, after the storm had cleared. Why not? I thought to myself. It was uncharacteristically warm, and a walk might help me feel better.

I ambled along in the sun's warmth, pushing Gracie in her stroller and watching Andrew pump his legs up and down on his Spiderman bike. Just ahead of me, Andrew put on his brakes, jumped off, and crouched down beside a patch of grass.

"Look, Mama, daisies!" Andrew shouted, amazed. I looked down where Andrew pointed and, sure enough, there was a beautiful patch of daisies. We hadn't noticed them before, even though we walked past this grass almost every day. Although all the other wildflowers had long succumbed to the parched landscape, the vibrant daisies flourished.

"How did they get there?" Andrew asked, as perplexed as I was.

I thought of "Consider the Lilies." The simple message in scripture and the beautiful song tell us that if God cares for the birds, flowers, and grass, He will care for us, too. My worries dissipated, and a slow smile formed on my face. For the first time in weeks, a new spark of hope flickered in my heart.

"Sometimes, it takes a little rain to breathe new life into something," I replied to my son's question.

And sometimes it takes a walk on an uncharacteristically warm day and a thriving patch of wild daisies to breathe new life into a doubting heart. That day, God reminded me once again that He cares for the lilies of the field, the daisies on the roadside—and my family and me.

My Prayer

Dear Father, thank you for blessings that abound even in times of drought. When my soul grows weary with the worries of this world, you continually renew it with a fresh perspective.

Amen.

The Dove

By Regina K. Deppert

"I said, Oh! That I had the wings of a dove! I would fly away and be at rest."
~Psalm 55:6

It was the morning before the funeral of my twenty-year-old son, Matthew. Nothing seemed real or right. I felt like I had stepped out of my body and was watching someone else go through the motions.

My mother, sister, brother, and I were in my living room when my brother noticed a mourning dove fluttering its wings at the patio door. It seemed to be looking directly at me. Even in my grief-induced stupor, I was drawn to it. It was making direct eye contact with me and cooing, as if calling me. The four of us froze in place, realizing this was not just an ordinary bird. Time seemed to stop. I slowly walked toward the patio doors, not wanting to frighten it away. The dove jumped onto the back of a chair where it would be closest to me, and kept cooing its sweet song and maintaining eye contact. I walked to within two feet of the dove.

When I got as close as I could, my knees buckled. I felt warm all over, as if someone had poured warm water over me. Instantly, I felt an incredible sense of love and an overwhelming peace within me. In my spirit, I heard, "I am free, and I am at peace!" I sobbed with a multitude of emotions. Behind me, I heard my family sobbing quietly, too. Their spirits had also heard similar messages.

The dove stayed around the patio all that day and was still there the next morning as we prepared to attend the funeral. I believe that if my family had not been present when this occurred, I would have thought I had imagined it. The four of us bonded through this experience in a way that words cannot explain.

The message that God sent me through the dove gave me the strength to carry on. It confirmed to me that my son was in the arms of Jesus. It took away my fears and helped ease my pain. Five years later, I cling to the gift of the dove, the gift of God's presence, love, and comfort during the worst loss a person could ever endure.

My Prayer

*Thank you, Heavenly Father, for watching over
us. You always know exactly what we need and
when we need it. We are grateful for your love
and understanding. Thank you for the gift
of the dove, which reminds us of your precious gift
of eternal life.*

Amen.

44

The Rainbow Child

By Theresa Sanders

"You are the light of the world."
~Matthew 5:14

"Its bad news," my sister, Christie, told me over the phone. "Erik has epilepsy."

I blinked back tears. "Oh, honey, I'm so sorry."

"He's suffered so much," she continued, "and now this dual diagnosis. I guess we'll just have to take it day by day."

"Yes," I said. "And pray."

"And pray."

Her voice stayed with me long after our call. Steadfast in her care of Erik, her twenty-year-old son, my sister was forever his advocate. He would always be the love of her life.

Autistic and very low-functioning, Erik had retreated into his inner world at eighteen months old and not spoken since. He could now communicate basic needs via sign language, but this achievement was exceedingly hard won. There had been countless doctors, programs, and therapies; Erik was poked, prodded, and tested for many years. Through it all, Christie went to great lengths to preserve her boy's unique and gentle spirit. "I don't want his world to be gray," she once told me. "I want him to see rainbows."

Epilepsy had dealt them a crippling double blow, adding a whole new level of complexity to an already complicated affliction. What would Christie and her husband have to do to further care for their only child? Moreover, how could they communicate what epilepsy even was to a young man who couldn't communicate? Erik's seizures must have terrified him. I wished for a way to help, but living nearly a thousand miles away made that impossible.

And then I recalled how Christie and I had ended our conversation, on that invocation to pray. All at once, it seemed the best thing I could do. I set about it the very next morning. As time passed, my prayers became more specific, focusing expressly on Erik and his needs. I added a rosary when I knew he'd be undergoing something traumatic, like a doctor appointment or an adjustment of medication.

One day, as I finished my prayer, I noticed something. There, on the wall across from me, just beneath my back window, was a tiny yet lovely spectrum... a small rainbow. I had seen it before, but it now held special significance. Though fleeting, it seemed to appear when sunlight filtered in through the window at just the right angle, then passed through a mosaic candle holder displayed there. It suddenly occurred to me that light worked hard to produce that spectrum of color. It bent and twisted and refracted, but without the refraction, light couldn't be prismatic. Light, I concluded, must be very brave. Just like Erik and his parents.

Sometimes, situations are simply bigger than we are, and all we can do is face them courageously. Yet if we can arm ourselves with prayer, our days don't feel quite so gray. And sometimes, amidst all the bending and twisting, all the refraction, we are graced with pure light and the presence of a rainbow child.

My Prayer

Illness and disability are never easy, Father, but help us to remember that you are the Supreme Healer, the pure and abundant light that brightens our way. Let us look for you not in the grand sweep of sameness, but in the fine and mysterious detail of the unique. When our days are gray and our spirits low, remind us of rainbows.

Amen.

45

More Than a Stranger

By Terry Ann Johnson

Do not forget to show hospitality to strangers, for by so doing some people have shown hospitality to angels without knowing it.
~Hebrews 13:2

The morning began early for me with the gloom of my beloved Granny's funeral looming before me. Granny's solid reassurance on life was the glue that had always held me together. Her faith had sprung from her as easily as the air flowed around you. Her death would leave a huge gap in this dreary world, one that could never be filled.

After the funeral, my husband Lynn and I, with our two daughters, drove to the little store we owned. The afternoon crawled along at a snail's pace, but just before closing time, I spotted a scraggly, dirty man near the curb out front. A shiver ran up my spine as I looked at the long, dirty hair and threadbare, filthy trench coat of the stranger. Every once in a while, he'd glance over his shoulder at me, making me more nervous by the second. I rushed to find Lynn in the rear of the store. The look in his eyes told me he understood I was afraid, but I waited until we were alone to tell him about the stranger so we wouldn't scare the girls.

Life began to move in what seemed like slow motion as I watched Lynn walk toward the stranger. Gruffly, Lynn asked the stranger what he was doing. Leaning forward, I tried to hear every word, not wanting to miss a thing. As the stranger spoke, Lynn relaxed his body, and I moved closer to hear better. In a quiet voice full of emotion, the stranger said he was waiting for us to leave so he could search our trash for food. I heard the man whisper that he was hungry, and that was all I needed to hear. I rushed back inside to make two sandwiches and grab a carton of milk. My hands quivered with emotion as I handed my meager offering to the stranger.

Slowly, the mysterious man reached out his hands and placed one on my shoulder while accepting the food with the other. He spoke in a soothing whisper, "God will always be with you." The words seemed to vibrate through my very soul. My dear, sweet Granny had uttered those very words to me since I was a little girl. And I knew at that second she was sending me a message from the great beyond.

While the stranger took the food and headed toward town, Lynn and I walked arm in arm back to where our beautiful daughters waited. Barely five minutes passed before we regretted not doing more for the stranger. Rushing the girls into the car, we headed to find our mysterious stranger. We didn't see a single car or person as we headed down the highway. Soon, I spotted the empty milk carton with the sandwich trash next it, but there was still no sign of the stranger anywhere. Confused, we drove into town, carefully watching every step of the twenty-some miles for any sign of him, but there was just a deserted highway.

While shivers ran the length of my body, the tears began to flow again. I had felt from the moment I handed that poor, raggedy man my small offering of nourishment that he was far more than he appeared. Now, as I remember that moment in my life when I felt so alone and lost, I cling to that memory. What appeared as a beggar brought faith back into my life and revived my thirsty soul.

My Prayer

*Dear Heavenly Father, please help me remember
that the world is full of people in need. Allow me
to see the true soul that lies in the heart of all
people. Regardless of how they appear, they might
bless our lives in some unforeseen way.*

Amen.

46

Chicken Soup
for the Soul.

God in the Campfire

By Carol A. Gibson

"I am with you and will watch over you wherever you go..."
~Genesis 28:15

I sat watching sparks from our campfire leap and dance in the darkness of the woods, thinking I'd turn in soon since it was nine o'clock. Suddenly, I became aware of an unusual, absolute stillness in my soul. And, after a moment, came a certain realization that I was no longer married.

What was that all about? Of course, I was married. Jack was at our home in Pennsylvania. But I couldn't shake this feeling. It wasn't that I wondered if I was no longer married, I had an unshakeable knowing that I was no longer married.

I saw car headlights meander through the campgrounds. I wasn't surprised when the car stopped in front of our camper because something told me the driver was looking for me.

My father went out into the darkness, and I heard a muted conversation between him and another man. After a few moments, the car drove away.

"Carol," Dad said, struggling to steady his voice, "wake up the children and dress them. We must return to Pennsylvania. There's been an accident, and Jack has been hurt."

I felt like I had been knocked to my knees. I was afraid to hear the answer to my questions. "What kind of accident? How hurt?"

"All we know is that he was riding his motorcycle and was hit by an intoxicated, hit-and-run driver."

The drive back to Pennsylvania seemed endlessly long. We arrived at the hospital in the middle of the night and went directly to the emergency room where a young doctor sat down beside me.

"Mrs. Johnson," he began. It occurred to me there was a degree of pain in his eyes I had never seen in the eyes of a stranger before. I had to look away.

"I'm sorry to tell you that your husband passed away at nine o'clock tonight. We did everything we could to save him, but his injuries were too severe. Before he died, he asked for you and the children. I told him we were sending for you."

Now I understood why I knew I was no longer married.

The unshakable knowledge I had experienced at the campfire, I believe, was the severing of what had been a very real spiritual bond created by God that happy day when Jack and I had married five years earlier. It had existed since then. Now, severed by Jack's death, this bond was gone.

The weeks and months that followed weren't easy. Jack being taken away so suddenly gave us no chance to say goodbye, and I missed him terribly.

But through it all, I was comforted and supported by knowing this: Who but someone as close as a spiritual husband could whisper campfire truths into my soul to help prepare me for news like that? And who but God could have given me the certain knowing I had experienced, so that I would be assured, when the time came, that He was already there in this tragedy before I was aware of it, walking through it with me?

My Prayer

Father, thank you for the ways in which you show us that even before we know our lives are touched by trouble, you are already there to comfort and strengthen us. By this example, help our faith grow so that, whether or not we sense your presence, we can know that you are with us always and in all things.

Amen.

Signs of David

By Laurie Kolp

Even though I walk through the valley of the shadow of death, I will fear no evil, for you are with me; your rod and your staff, they comfort me.
~Psalm 23:4

I was dyeing Easter eggs with my children when I got the call on March 22, 2008. "Laurie, this is Brad. There's no easy way to say this, but Stacy's dead. She shot herself today..."

Wa-wa, wa-wa, wa-wa. The words sounded as muffled as the teacher's voice in *Peanuts*. My heart became a trombone. I went numb. How could my best friend be gone?

After Stacy's death, there was a void in my life. We had spent almost every day together while our kids were in school. I found it difficult to eat and perform my daily duties as wife and mother. I was depressed.

Several Saturdays later, I drove over to my church and sat outside in front of the statue of the Virgin Mary. Spring flowers decorated the grounds, but all I saw was gray.

"Dear God, please give me a sign that Stacy's all right. I need to know she is with you. Help me get through this difficult time," I cried.

Suddenly, a cool breeze gently fanned my teary face. It was not a windy day. I felt compelled to go inside the church and pray. After kneeling for several minutes, I had an intuitive thought to walk over to the priest's confessional room. Surprisingly, the door was open.

I sat down in front of the welcoming priest and began to sob uncontrollably. I told him the story of Stacy's death, her heartache, and our unique friendship.

"God must have sent me here to talk to you. I feel so much better now," I said.

The priest took my hands and leaned closer to me.

"I feel the presence of a spiritual being from a different plane in this room today."

He paused. I glanced up and noticed his eyes were closed.

"Stacy needs your prayers. Whenever you are sad, pray for her. Remember the conversations and special times you shared. She will live on in your heart and memories."

I could still help Stacy through prayer? I felt like a swaddled newborn being comforted by my father. Hope filled the hole in my heart.

Later that night, as I thought about my visit with the priest, I remembered a conversation Stacy and I once had about the name "David." Everyone named David in her life was special—her father, brother, a mutual friend. They reminded her of David from the Bible, forever seeking God's will.

A tingling sensation flowed through my body. It was as if a current of electricity spread peace within. The priest I had spoken with that day was named Father David! I knew it was no coincidence. God had sent me into the church so that Father David could comfort me. I asked, and He answered. I bowed my head in gratitude.

My Prayer

God, thank you for sending me signs that I am not alone. Help me to recognize these extraordinary "God-incidences" in my life, thus allowing my aching heart to heal.

Amen.

48

Chicken Soup for the Soul

A Lunch to Remember

By Herchel E. Newman

The Lord gives strength to his people; the Lord blesses his people with peace.
~Psalm 29:11

Having completed our luncheon date, we encountered three middle-aged ladies while exiting the dining area. My wife, Lonnie, smiled and offered a greeting. I quipped, "We tried to wait on you, but decided to go ahead and dine." As the friendly giggling ceased, one turned to me and said, "You can still pay the bill if you like," serving up more laughter.

Receiving my change at the register while Lonnie used the restroom, a voice in my head said, "Go ahead." I rolled a ten, a five and some ones up in my hand and located their table. I was already enjoying the look I imagined would be on their faces. Their conversation ceased as I breeched their personal space. I leaned over the table and spoke slowly, "A random act of kindness." I released the contents of my hand and began walking away while their eyes were drawn to the wad of green.

"Wait, wait! Come back!" they chorused.

Grinning, I waved and kept going. But the farther away I got, the louder they called. Embarrassed, I returned to the table just to silence them. Before I could speak, however, the lady sitting on the lone side of the table scanned my face without a blink and asked, "What's your name?"

"Herchel," I replied solemnly.

"Herchel, give me your hand."

It sounded as much like an order as a request. She cradled my hand in hers and began to pray. It was her humbling words, not her grip, which held me fast. At her "Amen," the younger of the remaining two ladies said, "Now give me your hand."

Her hold was gentler. Her prayer targeted my health and wealth, hopes and dreams, family, influence and successes. She prayed loud and long as I stood in the narrow aisle, bent over the table.

Then the eldest lady spoke. "I arrived from California yesterday. Doctors said I should come to see my mother right away. I talked with her last night, but I don't know if she's given her life to the Lord. I've been stressed and weak with worry. I prayed through the night for us both and asked the Lord to please give a sign to comfort me. As the night wore on, I held hope that He would.

"These kind ministers said we should come here for breakfast before going to the hospital. You are the first person who has made personal contact with me today. You, Sir, are a God-send, for this has been no random act. I have the peace I asked for."

My Prayer

*Dear Lord, give us eyes that see, ears that hear,
and hearts that care. Grant us the courage to
follow your path wherever it may lead. But, most
of all, may your light be reflected in my eyes and
let others see your love in my actions.*

Amen.

49

Chicken Soup for the Soul

Eye to Eye

By Judi Folmsbee

He heals the brokenhearted and binds up their wounds.
~Psalm 147:3

The sun felt warm on my face that day. With autumn in full swing, leaves of every shade of orange, yellow, and purple surrounded me in our backyard. Neighboring fields, lawns, and porches displayed big orange pumpkins. The temperature was just right to work in the yard. I tore out the tomato and pepper plants from our raised bed garden. Even though many were still growing, summer was over for me. I decided to take a break and sat down on the bench in our yard by the Memorial Stone in memory of my husband, Rick. It's my favorite place to talk to him. Fourteen months earlier, he had died suddenly from a heart attack.

We enjoyed our beautiful backyard, especially in the fall. Rick always felt at home there. He would often say, "I don't need to take a vacation and go somewhere; I can do it right here."

As I sat there in the glorious sunshine, thinking about the anniversary we wouldn't be celebrating in November, memories of our almost thirty-nine-year marriage flooded over me. A penetrating loneliness wrapped around me, bringing an unexpected sob. Even though it had been more than a year since Rick's death, his absence was still hard to handle. Once again, I asked, "God, why did you take my best friend and wonderful husband? If only you could give me some assurance that Rick is in heaven." Since Rick was a devoted Christian, I knew in my head he was with the Lord, but my heart ached. I felt so alone and insecure.

I tried to remember all the things we used to do. Rick had positioned a hummingbird feeder behind the bench where I was sitting. We loved to watch the hummingbirds buzz through our yard. They would race after each other as if playing tag, releasing little chirp-chirp sounds. We called it Hummingbird Wars.

There aren't any hummingbirds still around, I thought. They have migrated to a warmer place.

Just then, a hummingbird came right up to my face, eye to eye. It got so close, I was startled at first. It hovered in front of me, weaving back and forth, with its eyes staring right into mine. "Thank you, Rick," I said, and the hummer took off.

The hummingbird was God's answer to my prayer and a way for Rick to let me know he was okay. The sun suddenly seemed even more glorious.

My Prayer

*Father, your blessings come in all shapes and
sizes. Fill my vision today with your beautiful
creation so I might witness a tiny glimpse of loved
ones who have passed.*

Amen.

From One Father to Another

By Kevin Morrison

"I sought the Lord and he answered me; He delivered me from all my fears.
Those who look to him are radiant; their faces are never covered with shame."
~Psalm 34:4-5

"I think the baby is gone." Those six solemn words from my wife at 5:00 A.M. sent my mind into a disorienting spin of confusion, sadness, and anger. We sat on the end of the bed before the sun came up, talking and crying. Then, for a long while, we said nothing at all. Only a few days earlier, we had called all of our friends and family around the country to share the good news. We were expecting our first child! We couldn't bear the thought of the phone calls we would now have to make.

We had all the baby name books, the parenting books, and even a tiny baseball outfit and glove I bought the day we found out about our coming child. The pregnancy and thoughts of our growing family took center stage in our lives. That morning, the spotlight suddenly turned to heavy darkness. We drove to the doctor, still holding an ounce of hope that we might be wrong. We hoped the doctor would tell us our baby was alive and we had nothing to worry about. Instead, he confirmed our fears. And, in that instant, the world became an unfair, unforgiving, and unkind place.

That cold, clear night, as my wife slept, I went for a walk to nowhere in particular. I sat down against a neighbor's car door. My head hurt, and my heart cried. I had no words for God yet, but I turned my eyes to the stars to look at Him. With my teary eyes, I asked for help, much like I had imagined my little child might ask for help in times of sadness. God answered my cry.

He gave me a vision, and I rushed home to draw it. An angel with our precious baby in his arms flew with all speed into heaven to deliver our child into the waiting embrace of Jesus. It was a beautiful sight and a beautiful baby. I am a terrible artist, but God helped me draw that vision. And when it was complete, I knew my baby was in great care, and we would indeed meet one day. Only hours earlier, I thought I had been robbed of that opportunity. God understood my pain as a father. In that vision, He gave me the peace I needed to live my life.

I have since been blessed with four amazing children. I thank God every day for each one of them, and then I thank Him for watching over my first baby. I don't know why He took that child home early, but I know His blessings for me and my family are abundant beyond measure. In my time of great sorrow, God shared a vision with me of the great happiness of my child entering heaven. And He has shown me that He has plans of prosperity for me and my family, even before we leave the womb. In my deepest sorrow, I looked to God, who revived me once again.

My Prayer

*Thank you, God, for your open arms in my times
of sadness, for your peace in my times of fear, and
your assurance in my times of uncertainty. As
your hands have been in my life, I pray that you
would use me in the lives of others, that through
me, those who might suffer would see you and
your unending love.*

Amen.

51

A Message in the Sky

By Dayle Allen Shockley

The LORD is close to the brokenhearted
and saves those who are crushed in spirit.
~Psalm 34:18

One evening, feeling anxious and longing for solitude, I stepped out into a quiet October night and walked to the towering pine in my front yard. Slumping down onto the cool ground, I pulled my legs close for warmth. Overhead, the sky stretched wide like a dark blanket as sounds of the night swirled around me.

The past few months had been filled with unspeakable sadness. At forty-seven, my sister found herself facing an unwanted divorce, ending a marriage of twenty-six years—a marriage nobody ever expected to end, and for reasons that could only be described as heartbreaking.

Since hearing the news, not a day had gone by that I didn't find myself overcome with grief. I pleaded with God to change hearts and minds, but it appeared the heavens were brass.

I'm not sure what I expected on this particular night, but an urgency consumed me as I sat there. I needed an answer. I had to know that God was still out there listening.

"Where are you, Lord?" I said, my words coming out in desperate sobs. "I need to know that you are with me in all of this turmoil and grief. I need to know that you hear me. Can you hear me, God? I need to know!"

My frantic plea floated across the lawn and faded into the night. I waited, anxious for a sign. A bird singing. A wind chime catching the breeze. Something indicating that God had heard me.

But there was only silence of the deepest kind.

With a heavy heart, I leaned back against the trunk of the pine and closed my eyes, letting the tears fall. I don't remember how long I sat there, but I will never forget what happened next.

When I opened my eyes, there, suspended in the blue heavens directly in front of me, framed perfectly between the branches of a neighbor's tree, was what appeared to be the biggest diamond I had ever seen.

An enthusiastic observer of the heavenly bodies, I knew immediately that it was the magnificent Venus. Though it's often called the morning and evening "star," Venus is not a star at all. Venus is a planet—the most brilliant planet in the solar system, so brilliant it can often be seen in daylight hours.

Had I been sitting two inches to the left or to the right, I would have missed this sight altogether. But there it was—Venus, flickering in a stunning display of colors. Its light entered my grief and took my breath away.

I knew it was God's gift to me—the sign I had longed for—because, for the first time in a long time, I felt Him there, filling the vast space around me. And I sensed that He was reassuring one of his despondent children: I am here, dear child. Morning and evening, I will always be here.

My Prayer

*Lord, your light will guide us safely through the
dark places in life. When things seem hopeless,
please help us wait for your subtle answers. For
you hear the cries of all your children and are
readily at hand when we need you most.*

Amen.

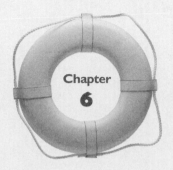

Chapter
6

*Devotional Stories
for
Tough Times*

His Healing Grace

*Then your light will break forth like the dawn,
and your healing will quickly appear.*

~Isaiah 58:8

52

Chicken Soup for the Soul

Treasures in the Attic, Treasures in Heaven

By Phyllis Cochran

"Forget the former things; do not dwell on the past.
See, I am doing a new thing!"
~Isaiah 43:18-19a

ive-year-old Jessica burst through the living room door. "What are you doing, Granny?" she asked, leaning over my arm.

"I forgot you were coming today," I said. How would I explain to Jessica that I was sorting through an old box of cards sent to our daughter, Susan, from her second-grade classmates years ago? Susan had fallen seriously ill at age seven and died two years later from a brain tumor. Jessica had heard about her mom's older sister over the years.

Purposefully, I had hidden Susan's mementoes in the attic where they would be protected—untouched by others. I thought of the cards as "my box of love." Several times I had attempted to throw away the get-well greetings, but ended up mourning for what could never be.

"What are you doing?" Jessica asked again. "Where did you get all these?"

"The cards were sent to your Aunt Susan when she was sick. I'm sorting them. You can help, Jess. I'll pass you the ones for the trash."

"Look at the yellow daisy. You can't throw this one away. It's too pretty," she insisted after I handed her the first.

"Set some aside for yourself," I said.

A few hundred cards later, Jess's sack was overflowing. The one for disposal remained empty. Jess latched onto an orange block in the bottom of the box. It bore the words SUSAN'S BLOCK in black lettering.

"Can I keep this?" Her brown eyes sparkled as she admired the bits of colorful fabric and buttons glued in a collage-like manner.

"Take this," I said, handing her another purple-painted craft.

"No, I want the orange one," she insisted, tugging on the wooden object.

"But, Jessica, orange was Susan's favorite color, and her name is on it," I said, grasping the chunky object. "What would you want it for?"

"I'll take it to show-and-tell. Then I'll put it on my desk."

I loved my grandchildren and would give them almost anything. But this? This was Susan's last creation. Carefully, I set the block aside.

Jess looked down in disbelief.

Inwardly, I struggled. I knew Susan had gone on before us to heaven. She no longer needed attic treasures. Letting go of this craft could never bring Susan back. I would never forget her. I was now storing up special memories with our grandchildren. The future and renewed happiness stood before me. I released the chunky wooden object into my granddaughter's hands.

The next day, Jessica showed Susan's block to her kindergarten class. For years, the orange block sat on Jessica's desk.

Each time I walked into Jessica's room and saw the wooden craft, I felt a renewed sense of joy. I had made the right decision.

My Prayer

Today, Lord, when I cling to attic treasures,
remind me to look to you and remember a new
generation has been given to us to enjoy. Help me
to hold dear those treasures of heavenly value.

Amen.

"My aunt who's in heaven made this, so I'm related to an angel!"

Reprinted by permission of Stephanie Piro ©2011.

53

Do You Believe?

By David Heeren

"... I am the LORD, who heals you."
~Exodus 15:26

The sudden pain struck with dagger force, twisting deep into my lower abdomen. I doubled over and had to steer the car to the side of the road. My wife, Joan, exchanged seats with me and drove us to the nearest hospital.

In the emergency room, between spasms of pain, I explained my symptoms to Joan. She was a registered nurse, so I asked her for a professional opinion. She told me it was likely that I had colitis.

I wondered: What if it's colon cancer?

It was late in the day when I was finally settled into a hospital bed. I lay there for many hours without being able to sleep. I was still experiencing pain, even though I had been given a painkiller. But the thing that kept me awake was anxiety.

I am a Christian, and I believe in the power of prayer, but not until after midnight did it enter my head that I hadn't talked to God about my illness, whatever it was.

I began talking to Him, silently, in my conscious mind: "Lord, this is awful. I'm scared. I've never been this sick in my life."

I continued to pray, and then, suddenly, a thought occurred to me: "Do you believe I can heal you?"

The thought was in the first-person tense, as if someone else had established a presence in my mind, but it seemed to me that it was a thought of mine.

I answered the question affirmatively in my mind. And, immediately, another thought took its place: "Do you believe I want to heal you?"

I smiled over the fact that I seemed to be having a mental conversation with myself, but the smile was brief. This was a conversation, whether it was one-sided or two-sided, that I needed to take seriously.

"Yes, Lord," I said internally. "I have read the Bible. I know you are a merciful God. You have raised the dead. You have healed many sick people. So, why not me?"

Then, one more thought: "Do you believe I will heal you?"

I wrestled with this question for a long time before stating my answer succinctly: "Yes, Lord, I believe you will heal me."

And then I fell asleep.

When I awoke the next morning, my body was suffused by a feeling of serenity. The pain was gone. Medical technicians put me through a series of tests that day, but I knew how they would turn out. In the afternoon, when a doctor entered my room, he smiled and said what I was expecting to hear: "There is nothing wrong with you. You may go home."

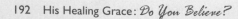

My Prayer

*Lord Jesus, you have been called the Great
Physician, and I believe you are. Thank you for
creating me and sustaining me, and for loving me
enough to heal my deepest fears and pains.*

Amen.

54

Marching in the Thought Parade

By Tracy Crump

"So I have been allotted months of futility, and nights of misery have been assigned to me. When I lie down I think, 'How long before I get up?' The night drags on, and I toss till dawn."
~Job 7:3-4

Every night was the same. I flipped restlessly in bed as thoughts paraded through my mind, no matter how hard I tried to stop them. The trouble was they never marched through and disappeared into the darkness. Oh, no. They made the corner and came round again and again in an endless circle, all centered on my mother.

Mom had suddenly begun to decline two months before. She became confused and forgetful. Cooking and driving were out of the question. Always an avid reader, she could no longer follow a story and stopped trying. More perplexing to me, however, were odd symptoms that didn't fit with the diagnosis of dementia the doctor handed down.

As a former nurse, my parents relied on me for medical advice. We had visited numerous specialists, yet Mom continued to deteriorate rapidly. Something else was wrong, but what? Every night, I tried to reason it through, exhausting myself with fruitless worrying.

"This is stupid!" I told myself as I watched the glowing clock tick the hours away each night. "Thinking won't change anything. Only God can handle this." I knew it, yet in that twilight stage between consciousness and sleep, I couldn't stop the thoughts from coming. Prayer was the obvious answer, but before a few words formed on my lips, my mind took off in other directions. "Maybe her thyroid is out of balance. Have we checked her for anemia lately?"

When I realized another hour had passed, I tried reciting scripture to halt the thought parade. "The LORD is my shepherd, I lack nothing. He makes me lie down in green pastures, he leads me beside quiet waters…" (Psalm 23:1-2). "Water. Mom doesn't drink enough water. Maybe she has a urinary tract infection. That always throws older people for a loop." And off I went again.

Every morning, shame would overtake me. I was supposed to trust in God with all my heart and not lean on my own understanding. That fact shone clear in the daylight, but in the dark, shadows obscured it again.

Finally, one night, I simply gave up. "Lord, there's nothing more I can do," I prayed. "Please forgive me for trying to play God." As I drifted off to sleep, the long-forgotten memory of a friend whose father had symptoms similar to Mom's floated into my consciousness. A few weeks later, my mother had surgery for normal pressure hydrocephalus, the condition that plagued both her and my friend's father. God gave me the answer I had tried so hard to devise on my own.

The Creator of the universe held the solution to my dilemma all along, but I had to concede defeat first. Only by putting myself completely in His hands could I hear His voice at last. Maybe next time I'll remember who holds all the answers and avoid nights of misery marching in the thought parade.

My Prayer

Creator God, only by trusting in you can I find the answers I seek. Please forgive me when I forget that and try to depend on my own reasoning to solve problems. It is comforting to know your thoughts are not my thoughts, nor are your ways my ways.

Amen.

55

Go by Faith

By Phyllis Cochran

"But he knows the way that I take;
when he has tested me, I will come forth as gold."
—Job 23:10

The autumn leaves were in full bloom when I drove toward the nursing home that October afternoon. I thought about Ruth, the sprightly ninety-one-year-old lady I had befriended. She had no family or visitors, so every Wednesday afternoon I dropped in to see her.

Just as I pulled into the parking lot and turned off the car, the familiar symptoms of an oncoming migraine headache erupted. For years, this ailment had rendered me useless for hours, even an entire day. I recognized the symptoms. The pattern never varied. A numbing sensation in my left arm warned me of an oncoming migraine. Next, tiny silver speckles would float in mid-air as my eyesight gradually blurred, leaving me with one-sided vision followed by an explosive pounding in my right temple.

Leaning back in the parked car, I tried to relax. How would I drive home like this? I'd be unable to see the road clearly. And the hammering in my head would make it unbearable to communicate with Ruth. I prayed, asking God for His help and guidance. Minutes passed, and I tried to remain calm, thinking that if I waited until the blurriness passed, I could drive home.

Then, deep within, a quiet voice seemed to say, "Go. Go by faith." The simple words with their intense direction twirled around in my mind. What did I have to lose? I decided to obey the inner voice and walk into the nursing home.

Ruth was reclining in a chair and staring into space. "Hello, Ruth. You probably thought I wasn't coming today," I said.

She greeted me with open arms. "I knew you'd come," she said, smoothing her skirt and folding her hands.

While she was talking, I tried to listen, but the blurred vision was progressing. My attention was not on our conversation but on the soon-to-be-thunderous pounding of the migraine.

In the middle of our conversation, I was stirred again by the words, "You are doing my will. I am healing your migraines." I tried to dismiss the most recent inner voice, but it remained.

Instead of reaching the stage of one-sided vision, my eyesight miraculously cleared. I expected the explosive throbbing to follow as usual. There was none. I drove home free from all symptoms, prepared dinner for my family, and never experienced the slightest sign of the tortuous head pain.

More than twenty years later, I am still free from migraine headaches. That afternoon, the Lord taught me to pray, sit quietly, and listen to His still, small voice within when I am faced with difficult situations. I'll always be thankful I trusted God's whisper to go—go by faith.

My Prayer

Whenever I am in a place, Lord, where I do not
know which way to turn, remind me to turn to
you. Only you can quiet my mind to listen to your
still, small voice within.

Amen.

56

Broken Dishes, Healing Hearts

By Jennie Bradstreet

"... Each of you is to take up a stone on his shoulder, according to the number of the tribes of the Israelites, to serve as a sign among you. In the future, when your children ask you, 'What do these stones mean?' tell them..."
~Joshua 4:5-7

For months, my husband Erik had been battling cancer. Nearing the end of his treatment, his pain had grown increasingly worse. Every movement caused excruciating pain, and noises—even happy ones—over-stimulated him. I was on constant guard to keep the kids quiet, but it was becoming an unreasonable expectation.

One specific night seemed worse than most. Parker, our nine-year-old son, had been badgering and irritating his eleven-year-old sister, eventually provoking her to act upon her redheaded temperament. I had interrupted and shushed arguments all night long when I finally blew my top. I didn't realize how much frustration was pent up inside of my son because he threw the mother of all temper tantrums. In horror, I watched as he threw himself to the floor, thrashing and screaming. I was very close to joining him in his meltdown when I heard God's quiet voice saying, "Let him break something. He's angry." Then the image of my kitchen dishes came to mind.

I ran to the kitchen and gathered as many plates, cups, and bowls as I could carry and went downstairs. With my arms full, I told Parker to follow me. With an angry sigh, he followed, probably expecting to be punished for his outburst. Instead, I handed him a plate, pointed at the wall, and said, "Throw it." He looked at me, raising his eyebrow, so I grabbed a cup and threw it against the wall. This time, he looked at me like I had lost my mind.

"Throw the plate," I repeated. With a tentative look and a sissy throw, he tossed it, not even breaking it. So I said, "Pick it up and really throw it. Smash it like you mean it." I picked up another dish and threw it. "I hate you, cancer!" I yelled.

Finally understanding what I was doing, Parker picked up the dish and chucked it hard. "I hate Dad being sick!" he yelled, smashing a plate against the wall. "You suck, cancer!" Another dish shattered. "I want my dad back." More shards of dishes littered the floor. And, finally, he shouted, "I don't want my dad to die!" He dissolved into tears.

Reaching the end of our rampage, we sat on the floor in the midst of all the pieces and cried. Relief flooded our hearts. The pressure valve released.

We ate from paper plates for a while. Our friends and family thought I was crazy for destroying every dish in my kitchen. I realize they only saw the "value" of my dishes, but that night was one that neither Parker nor I will ever forget. It was when he realized that I valued his emotions and wellbeing over any material thing in my house.

Shortly after this took place, I read Joshua 4:5-7: "Each of you is to take up a stone on his shoulder… to serve as a sign among you. In the future, when your children ask you, 'What do these stones mean?' tell them…" It sparked an idea.

A few months later, when Erik finished treatment and got back on his feet, Parker and I created a set of mosaic stepping stones from the broken dishes. And someday, when he has a home of his own, I will give him one so he will always have a reminder of the healing that took place that night.

My Prayer

*Lord, many times our children suffer when bad
things happen to us here on Earth. Guide and
protect them in every moment of every day so
that they may know you are near.
In your loving name…*

Amen.

"Go ahead and smash them... that's why God made paper plates!"

Reprinted by permission of
Stephanie Piro ©2011.

57

The Comfort of Each Other

By Michele Cushatt

Praise be to the God and Father of our Lord Jesus Christ,
the Father of compassion and the God of all comfort,
who comforts us in all our troubles, so that we can comfort those
in any trouble with the comfort we ourselves receive from God.
~2 Corinthians 1:3-4

My phone buzzed with an incoming text: "Laura was in a snowboarding accident. She's in the hospital. Please pray."

I stared in disbelief at the message. In a few bland characters, I learned my dear friend was seriously injured. But a glance out the window showed the predicted snowstorm raging in earnest. Large flakes swirled in circles in my backyard. Now was not the best time for a blizzard. But snow or no snow, I had to go. What are friends for if not to weather the worst of life together?

Within the hour, I threw a packed bag into my truck. After exchanging hugs with my husband and children, I backed out of the garage and began a slow trek into the mountains. The blowing snow moved in horizontal lines in front of me, obscuring the roads and fighting me for control.

Soon, darkness fell, and exhaustion settled in. The weeks before had been some of the most difficult I'd faced. A move from our family home, economic challenges, the death of another dear friend, and struggles with our teenagers had replaced peace with tension. During one difficult night, I'd called Laura, desperate for the reassurance of a friend. I spilled my heartache over the phone while she listened, allowed me to cry, and told me she loved me and would always be there for me.

Now, as I crawled over the mountain toward the hospital on the other side, I realized it was my turn to hold her hand, let her cry, and tell her I'd be there for her, as long as it took.

When I arrived, her smile lit up the room. With multiple broken bones, she could do little more than squeeze my hand and allow the tears to fall. Seeing her pain released my own.

"I'm with you, Laura, as long as it takes. We're going to get through this."

And we did. During part of her recovery, she lived in our home, a time so full of laughter, tears, friendship, and healing that I doubt its equal will ever be found this side of heaven. We talked from our breakfast coffee until long after my family retired to bed. We shared stories from childhood, wrestled with the challenges of adulthood, and laughed until her back couldn't bear it. And when either her physical pain or my heart pain became a mountain too big to climb, we soaked in each other's presence until we made it to the other side. And right there, in the middle of life's storms and my living room, we experienced the comfort of each other.

Challenges will still come, storms seemingly too violent to weather, mountains appearing too steep to scale. Every struggle conquered leaves others waiting in line to take its place. But we don't have to live it alone. Thank God, we don't have to live it alone.

My Prayer

Thank you, Father, for the comfort you give us through others. Teach us to follow your ways and become a source of strength for those who are also suffering. Let us celebrate the gift of community that you have given us.

Amen.

58

Chicken Soup for the Soul

Here's to You, Grandpa!

By Mary Z. Smith

The Levites calmed all the people, saying, "Be still, for this is a holy day. Do not grieve." Then all the people went away to eat and drink, to send portions of food and to celebrate with great joy, because they now understood the words that had been made known to them.

~Nehemiah 8:11-12

My father-in-law passed away from lung cancer. At ninety-two, Mom could no longer live alone, so she came to live with us. We managed to get through the sad weeks and months ahead by getting used to each other and the new living arrangements.

Still, we seldom spotted a smile on Mom's face.

Then our married daughters and their families paid us a visit. We got together one evening at a favorite restaurant we'd often frequented when Dad was still with us. I wondered if it would make Mom even sadder.

"It would probably be best not to bring up old memories," I thought to myself as we pulled into the parking lot.

After we'd gotten situated around a large oval table, our younger daughter raised her glass of iced water into the air.

"Here's to Grandpa, and the way he'd always ask to see the chef after a delicious meal," she toasted, clinking glasses with her husband, Greg.

"Remember the time he tried speaking in Italian to the waiter?" our older daughter piped up. "He ordered some strange dessert called 'baldino.' The poor waiter thought he was referring to his bald head."

I glanced across the table in time to see a smile creeping across Mom's wrinkled face.

"Remember the time he sneezed so loudly at the mall that it echoed across the food court? The entire room grew silent!"

"What about the time he couldn't hear the announcer's warning about a tornado alert and asked everyone why there was a TOMATO alert?"

Mom suddenly chuckled.

As I watched everyone wiping happy tears from their cheeks with linen napkins, I relaxed for the first time all evening.

Our food arrived. We continued reminiscing and sharing happy memories of a precious family member who would live on in our hearts forever.

I learned an important lesson from our youngest family member that evening. Sharing memories of a loved one can be a healing thing... a good thing even.

How would Dad have said it?

È una buona cosa! A good thing indeed...

My Prayer

*Father, if we raise our children to be godly, they
will teach us about your loving kindness at times
when we least expect it. Thank you for family and
for our love for each other.*

Amen.

A Hole in My Nest

By Helen L. Hoover

"... I will go to him, but he will not return to me."
~2 Samuel 12:23

"BANG!" The dreaded pistol shot rang out across the parking lot where our family waited. We had hoped the SWAT team could convince Gary his life was worth living, but they could not. The preceding week had whirled by as our older son and daughter, my husband Larry, and I tried to convince our troubled and depressed son/brother that he needed professional counseling and medication. Our worst nightmare materialized.

The death of a child is devastating to the parents, whether by suicide, accident, murder, war, or illness. Our children are supposed to grow up, have a productive adult life, and help us in our older years. They are to outlive us, not we them. We have hopes and dreams for their lives. But the life we foresaw for Gary had been shattered.

When a child dies, grief intermingles with unforgiveness, anger, denial, self-pity, regret, confusion, loss of hope, dread, misunderstanding, and a multitude of "whys." It is a path parents never choose, but are thrown into. I expected my nest to be empty in my older years, not with a hole in it caused by the death of a son.

Larry and I attended a grief support group and talked often with close confidants to work through the grief, which helped immensely.

But just when I think I've overcome all signs of grief, sadness sneaks up and overtakes me. In talking with other parents who have lost a child, grief—at various levels—seems to be a continual pathway.

His death left questions that only God can answer. Why didn't He intervene? Why did this have to happen? What was the purpose of Gary's untimely death? Could we have done anything different to change the outcome?

We haven't received any answers. But from sermons, the scriptures, and other Christians, we have received repeated assurances of God's love for His children, including Gary. Larry and I have resolved to continue trusting, obeying, serving, and loving God, even though we do not understand.

The hole is still in my nest as I miss Gary terribly, but I can enjoy life without him. God is faithful to help and comfort us as the days, months, and years go by. A joyous reunion will take place when I die and see Gary again in heaven, and the reasons for his untimely death will no longer matter.

My Prayer

Lord, thank you for the time you give us with our earthly children. Comfort us when they leave our lives and hearts too early. Please walk beside them until we meet again in heaven.

Amen.

The Garden

By Barbara Cueto

My beloved spoke and said to me, "Arise, my darling, my beautiful one, come with me. See! The winter is past; the rains are over and gone. Flowers appear on the earth; the season of singing has come, the cooing of doves is heard in our land."
~Song of Solomon 2:10-12

As I pulled up what seemed like the gazillionth weed from the overgrown garden and dug out yet another boulder, all at once it dawned on me why God had led me to do this.

I'd never considered myself a horticulturalist or a gardener or even thought I had a green thumb. The only things I'd really ever been good at were singing, acting, and occasionally writing. And I excelled at making mistakes. My life had been pretty miserable, much like this garden I was weeding, full of ugly, uninvited growth that didn't require much attention to spread. The dirt of my life hadn't been very fertile except to yield huge harvests of wasted plant life — weeds. And there had been plenty of rocks. Like the ones before me, with only a sliver visible above the topsoil, I'd never guessed how far down under the earth I'd have to dig in order to pull them out.

But now I was in rehab. I was going to my daily meetings with the same dedication I'd given my addictions to alcohol and drugs for decades. During the few short years my husband and I had lived in this house, I'd never taken any interest in the long garden area that stretched the entire length of our back fence. Of course, all of the problem areas in my life were grossly neglected. This part of my house was indicative of the larger part of my whole existence. I had let everything go. All my potential had been overwhelmed and covered up by the bad things that had happened to me. There were no more gardens in my life, only long strips of once-hopeful ground laden with rich weeds of bad memories and pain, along with enormous stones of worthless indulgence and fruitless pursuit.

However, with God's help, the necessary first steps toward freedom and wholeness were being forged, and I was doggedly taking every day one at a time. And certainly each new dawn brought a new and distinct challenge. Every hour that I was clean and sober was another mountain I'd summit. Naturally, all of my old compulsions would need to be replaced with new diversions. And that was how, one bright spring day, I looked out back and saw the possibility of a flowing garden in the barren plot.

Every day, I worked tirelessly, pulling up weed after weed and unearthing more rocks than I could have imagined hidden there. And I went to my recovery meetings and did the same — pulling out the old and replacing with the new. I could see now where every rock had taken up so much room in the garden that there was no place for the roots of the good plants to grow. But now my beautiful seedlings would have plenty of space to stretch and flourish.

I planted every imaginable flower of every shape, size, and color of the rainbow in my garden. And I grew, too. Even as the plants patiently, eventually awakened to reveal their new blooms, so did my soul. My neighbors, who had seen me laboring night and day, came to admire my handiwork. Likewise, I stood and watched, awestruck by the magnificent blossoms in the new garden God had planted in my heart.

My Prayer

*God, what a truly wonderful world you have
created. You are the master gardener and know
all the weeds that plague our lives and souls.
Pluck from me anything that is barren and
fill my heart only with things that are beautiful
in your sight.*

Amen.

61

Hidden Things of the Heart

By Cyndi S. Schatzman

He reveals deep and hidden things;
he knows what lies in darkness, and light dwells with him.
~Daniel 2:22

Driving down the road, I was suddenly overcome with the feeling that my husband was going to die. How could this premonition be true? Todd had played competitive rugby for more than ten years and was still exercising regularly. Was this fear speaking or was it the Lord? I started praying that God would open my eyes to which it was.

I started noticing little symptoms: a nap after his run, pale coloring, less energy, and more coffee. All told me there was a problem. The Lord also brought to my mind an event almost seventeen years earlier as I lay on Todd's chest. As a critical care nurse in a heart transplant unit, I thought I heard a murmur. After a visit to the doctor, I was told that nothing was wrong and to "stop playing nurse." But something never really sat right with me.

Shortly after Todd's medical appointment so long ago, our son, Carson, was born blue-faced with four heart defects. We waited anxiously until he had surgery at six months of age. With no family history, the doctors just assumed it was a random event. It seemed ironic to me that being a cardiac nurse, my own son had heart issues. The years passed, and Carson grew into a healthy, strong, sports-playing teenager.

With my head back on Todd's chest so many years later, once again hearing a murmur, I said, "I am not asking this time; I'm telling your doctor to schedule an EKG." After three months of inconclusive tests, we finally saw what God had known all along: Todd had lived for forty-five years with a 1.3-cm hole in the upper chambers of his heart. The doctors were amazed that he had no symptoms. He most likely would have died exercising.

God had reached His mighty hand down from heaven and pointed to Todd's chest to reveal the hidden things of the heart. As we gathered our kids around the kitchen table to share the news, Carson said, "Dad, is this hereditary? Did I give this to you?" Todd replied, "Yes, it's hereditary, but it's probably the other way around."

After Todd's surgery, I felt something deep in my soul like never before—overwhelming gratitude for God's invisible hand of protection over my family. He was powerful enough to heal and strengthen Carson's heart. He was gracious enough to open my ears to the secret things of the heart that would have killed Todd. He gave me the desire to become a nurse at age five so I could later serve my family. God saved the lives of both my son and husband. His trustworthiness surrounded me like oxygen in the room. He was always there and always would be, whether I noticed or not, protecting, guiding, caring, and loving my family.

My Heavenly Father is doing some surgical work on my own heart as well. He is removing any doubt that He is present, powerful, and personal.

My Prayer

Thank you, my Heavenly Father, that you
know, you see, you protect, and you are ever
present in our lives. Thank you for your timing
in revealing the hidden things of our heart
physically, emotionally, and spiritually. We praise
you for shedding your light on the things that are
confusing to us, or where we feel "in the dark," for
we trust your presence to give us peace.

Amen.

62

Pain's Panacea

By Florence Crago

And a woman was there who had been subject to bleeding for twelve years,
but no one could heal her. She came up behind him and touched the edge of
his cloak, and immediately her bleeding stopped.
~Luke 8:43-44

On a Saturday evening, after a long, hard day of packing and driving, we arrived at our new home with our three young children and a trailer full of household items, clothing, etc. We were all dead tired, the kids were cranky, and my husband and I were faced with the task of preparing food and beds for us all. I was grateful that my recurrent toothache had not bothered me most of that day.

The dentist had told me that the cause of my excruciating toothache was a wisdom tooth pressing against the tooth next to it. It might need to be extracted in time, he said, or it might decide to lie dormant. While settling the kids for the night, my jawbone began to pound with pain as it had never done before. I tried everything—aspirin, a hot water bottle, an ice bag—with no relief. In an effort to escape the torture, I tossed and turned in bed that night, trying to stifle my crying so my husband could sleep.

Finally, in desperation, I prayed, "God, I've done everything I can to stop this pain. I don't even know where to find a dentist in this town and at this hour. Please, you take it! I don't think I can stand it any longer." Then I remembered the woman in the Bible who believed she would be healed if only she could touch Jesus's cloak. If only I could touch Jesus!

I must have passed out. Quite suddenly, God and I were standing together on a beautiful pink cloud in a lovely blue sky. I could not see His face, but I could feel His presence. It even seemed like His arm was around my shoulders. Together, we were looking at my writhing body on the bed. The searing pain was red, and it was interesting to watch as it dug into my jaw. Amazingly, I felt nothing of the pain.

Then it was morning. The pain was gone. I had had a refreshing sleep. Some may say that the medicines I'd taken had induced unconsciousness. Or that the tooth had reached the dormancy the dentist had referred to. It makes no difference to me. I'm convinced that God took that pain from me in a powerful moment of wordless communion with Him.

Thirty years later, the guilty tooth was extracted—not for any problem or because of pain, but simply because it was lying there, doing nothing.

My Prayer

Father, thank you for healing! I pray that I might know your presence in all my days and nights. And please forgive me if I ever doubt your willingness to help me in times when I reach the end of my rope.

Amen.

Chapter
7

Devotional Stories for Tough Times

Renewed Faith

No discipline seems pleasant at the time, but painful. Later on, however, it produces a harvest of righteousness and peace for those who have been trained by it.

~Hebrews 12:11

63

The Darkness in My Heart

By Dianne E. Butts

"You have heard that it was said to the people long ago, 'You shall not murder, and anyone who murders will be subject to judgment.' But I tell you that anyone who is angry with a brother or sister will be subject to judgment..."
~Matthew 5:21-22

had a right to be angry, and I knew it. Already, I had lived a couple of years without my brother while the man who had killed him walked free.

I remember seeing that man the night of the crash. He seemed to care little that he had driven drunk, causing the crash. A year later during the civil trial, his attorney tried to make it look like it was all my brother's fault. My brother had too much to drink, too, he said. The headlight on his motorcycle was not functioning, he said. Lab tests refuted those claims. The whole time, that man said little.

I wanted him to be sorry. I wanted him to say he was sorry. I didn't get what I wanted. And my anger simmered and grew and boiled and threatened.

He continued with his life. My family tried to continue without my brother.

As time passed, I found myself wishing bad things on that man.

Maybe something bad would happen to him. When nothing bad happened, my frustration grew. Didn't he deserve it? Where was God? Was there no justice?

Then one dark night, I imagined myself getting my revenge.

It didn't bring me comfort. Instead, it brought me terror. Was I actually capable of such dark thoughts and disturbing wishes? I was shocked at how dark my mind had become, and more shocked at how it had colored my whole life. My anger revealed itself in my attitudes and actions, coloring my dreams and my whole life in ever-darkening shades.

I can't remember how it came about, but somehow God made His Word known in my mind. I heard Jesus's words that I would be subject to judgment, and I saw with sudden clarity how guilty I was. I had allowed my heart to wander so far that I had actually wished death on that man, and I cared little that I felt that way. I wasn't sorry.

With equal clarity, I suddenly saw that the forgiveness Christ wanted me to extend to the man was not for his sake, but for my own. My anger wasn't hurting him; it was only hurting me. Forgiving him was not letting him off the hook for what he had done. Forgiving him meant my own anger would not eat me alive from the inside out.

In the decades since, I've actually found myself praying for that man. I don't know where he is now or what he has done with his life since then, but my hope is that God somehow made His Word known to him, and that he has come to know the Savior. If the Lord ever causes our paths to cross again, I'd like to be able to tell him about Jesus, and that His forgiveness of my sins has made all the difference in my life.

My Prayer

Father, when we are angry at someone because of their sin, remind us that our own sins are just as big in your sight. Help us understand that if we refuse to forgive others, we really haven't grasped how much you have forgiven us for our own mistakes. You are the only way that leads to life eternal.

Amen.

64

Chicken Soup for the Soul

Kindness with finesse

By Ann McArthur

*A bruised reed he will not break, and a smoldering wick he will not snuff out,
till he has brought justice through to victory.*
~Matthew 12:20

I am grieved to say there was a time in my life when I was living in rebellion against God. I had come to a crisis, and rather than trusting God, my faith utterly failed, and I went the wrong way. This way led downward and finally to homelessness. Unable to find work, I lived in a borrowed car and had little to eat. I was the prodigal in the pigpen. My suffering—all of it deserved—was intense: the gnawing loneliness, the emptiness of my days with nothing to do, the shattering of self-confidence. I even failed at suicide.

One suffocatingly hot summer's evening, feeling emotionally fragile yet desperately homesick for God, I got up the courage to slip into a church service. Acutely aware that I was dirty and inappropriately dressed, I sat in the back. I had planned to sneak out quickly when the service was over so that I wouldn't have to talk to anybody, but the pastor met me at the door.

"How nice to have you visit with us," he said, shaking my hand warmly. "I'm so glad you came."

I could hardly believe that anybody would be so courteous and respectful to someone in my condition. "Thank you," I mumbled, my face flaming.

"What is your situation? Is there anything you need?"

"No, not really." I didn't mean to brush off his question, but I didn't know how to respond to such unexpected concern. I took a step toward the door, but he put his hand on my shoulder.

"Do you have a place to sleep tonight?" he asked quietly.

As embarrassed as I was, I couldn't bring myself to lie to him. "Only my car," I admitted.

I was astonished by what happened next. This kind man gave me a key to the church. He told me to sleep in the church nursery so I could use the air conditioning and to cook in the church kitchen until I could get on my feet. Instead of treating me with disdain, he treated me with dignity and the confidence that I would get on my feet. He gave me hope.

That night as I settled down on a crib mattress on the floor in the cool nursery, I felt assurance that I was still accepted as a child of God. My Heavenly Father was welcoming me home.

Thanks to God and this pastor, I did find a job eventually and got back on my feet — both financially and spiritually.

My Prayer

Dear God, thank you for extending grace to us, often when we least deserve it. You treat the battered and bruised with such gentleness. Your graciousness is kindness with finesse.

Amen.

65

Chicken Soup for the Soul®

He Never Left Me

By Sandy Lackey Wright

I will not leave you comfortless, I will come to you.
~John 14:18

A numb exhaustion permeated every activity. Daily, I had to scrape myself out of bed. My child wasn't the only thing that had died.

The sun was too bright, but I went outside anyway. Agitated, I paced back and forth, glaring at the fall sky. Tears streamed, and then grief welled so strongly that I stumbled and had to grab the rail. My world wove and buckled around me. From lungs that felt crushed, I gasped for air. My primal scream, then a soulful groan, startled me. I doubled over, crumbling to the ground and sobbing until I could cry no more.

Fear plagued me. It was a fear of what God would ask me to do next. Exhausted, I looked up to my God, with whom I had talked daily, and asked—no, demanded—Him to leave. For an instant, I felt my body cradled—then there was a strong pulling away. I was empty, but I didn't care.

Everything about my life unraveled. For four years, I had struggled to keep our youngest alive. Now there was no purpose for my life. My misery was so deep that I believed my other two children, ages twelve and eight, no longer needed me. I wished to die. This deadness went on for two years. And in all that time, not once did I ask God to come back.

Then one day, in my church's parking lot, I heard God speak. He said that two ladies were sitting at a table inside the church. I was to talk to them. I looked around, but no one was there. I slowly opened the door to the church and then froze. Two women were indeed sitting at a table. Hidden, I pressed against the wall, but I knew deep inside that if I did not obey, I would spiritually die.

Slowly, I walked halfway to the women and stopped. I asked what they were doing. They said they were praying for a director for a children's musical. I blanched, but found myself telling them I had directed plays and would be happy to help them find someone. Their eyes got big. "No, no, no. YOU are our director."

God showed me something that day. Though I had rejected Him, He had never left me. He still held me in the palm of His loving hand. I did not plead for Him to come back to me. Instead, he wooed me to Him. He knew I was ready. Mark Twain said, "Drag your thoughts away from your troubles... by the ears, by the heels, or any other way you can manage it." With God's love, I did.

My Prayer

Thank you, Father, for staying with us in our
intense trials and never letting us go.
I thank you that I don't have to go it alone;
you are always with me.

Amen.

66

God's Great Bear Hug

By Karen C. Talcott

Get rid of all bitterness, rage and anger, brawling and slander, along with every form of malice. Be kind and compassionate to one another, forgiving each other, just as in Christ God forgave you.
~Ephesians 4:31-32

"God, how could you be so cruel?" I yelled into the air. "Do you really care about me or is this religion stuff all just a hoax?"

I waited for an answer, a sign that God had heard me and was there to comfort me. But the only thing I felt around me was my pain and heartache. The funeral for my mother was still too fresh in my mind to ponder.

Sitting alone in my apartment, my mind replayed the past few years. First, my father had been stricken with cancer. He fought a valiant fight, but he only survived eight months after his diagnosis. Soon afterward, my mother received the news that her breast cancer had recurred. She too didn't take this dreaded disease lying down, but the end results were the same. The two people I needed, cherished, and loved most in the world were suddenly stripped from my life, and I was left alone. It seemed cruel, and I wasn't afraid to rage at God for my loss.

I sat there for a long time in the darkness. Nothing in my life made sense anymore. Over time, the anger slowly seeped out of me, but numbness took its place. I decided that I didn't want to be in a relationship with God. I stopped all my church activities and found things to do on Sunday mornings. I slept in, read the paper, and even went to breakfast. Filling my life with these activities dampened the pain, and I thought life was slowly returning to normal.

But, to my surprise, I woke one Sunday morning with a feeling of unease. Pacing around my apartment, an inner battle began to rage. Did I want to keep living my life like this or was it time to return to God? Still without a clear heavenly answer, I decided to attend the morning church service. I was now running late, which suited me fine as I slipped into the back row unnoticed. As I sat through the service, my heart began to thaw just a little. It wasn't a huge, noticeable shift, but for the first time in many months I didn't feel so angry.

Returning to my apartment, my heart and mind were at war. I was torn between holding onto my grudge with God or letting it go and starting fresh.

"God, can you take on a battered Christian?" I asked. "Do you really want me back after I blamed you for the deaths of my parents?"

There was silence for a moment, but then almost like a movie was being played out in my head, I saw a father throw everything aside as he ran toward his wayward son. He pulled him into a tight bear hug, and they stood embracing for a long time. The father whispered something into his son's ear, and a deep look of understanding passed between them.

The scene disappeared from my vision, but I knew this prodigal son message was heaven-sent. My bitterness was forgiven, and my true Father was welcoming me back. So I did the only thing I knew how—I put my arms around my Father and simply hugged Him back.

My Prayer

Dear Heavenly Father, how I must test your patience and love for me. Forgive me when I blame you for the unfortunate events in my life. I thank you for your deep, abiding love that always welcomes me back.

Amen.

67

Chicken Soup for the Soul

Healing Tears

By Christa Holder Ocker

*For he has not despised or disclaimed the suffering of the afflicted one, he has
not hidden his face from him but has listened to his cry for help.*
~Psalm 22:24

The shrill ring of the phone awakens me. I raise myself up on
one elbow and reach for the receiver.

"Hello?"

"Hey, Mom, whatcha doing?" Peter's voice is like a warm embrace
in the chill morning air. "Want to come over?"

"What time is it?" I sink back into my pillow, still half asleep.

He ignores my question and continues with masterful persuasion. "Come for breakfast... I'm making blueberry pancakes... Paula
loves blueberry pancakes," he adds as an afterthought. Paula, a beautiful girl from Laos, is Peter's wife. Peter and Paula have four children—three girls and one boy—striking Eurasian-mix kids, happy
and vivacious.

"So, hurry up and come, okay?" Peter's voice warms my heart.
This child of mine is special. From the day he was born, his infectious
smile and generous spirit warmed everyone around him.

"Sure, honey," I mumble in my still dreamy state, but then I wake
with a start. The golden feeling of sun turns black like thunder as
reality sets in. Peter is dead.

When Peter passed away a few years ago, I wanted to die, too. I found no solace in my husband or other three children. I found no solace in nature. I found no solace in prayer. Instead of sorrow, I felt only anger and hate. I hated everything and everyone. But most of all, I hated God. I shook my fist at Him and shouted, "How can you be so cruel?"

Seasons came, and seasons passed. I walked through life with a rock in my heart. But then, one morning when the clouds hang low and threaten to weep, the telephone rings.

"Hello?"

"Hey, Grandma, whatcha doing?" Katie's voice is like a warm embrace in the chill morning air. "Can you come over?" Katie is Peter's youngest child—child of my child, so much like my child. "Maybe we can go to Nancy's and pick apples, okay?" she continues with masterful persuasion. Nancy, a neighbor and friend, lives next to her brother's apple orchard.

"That's an excellent idea, sweetheart," I reply.

"Okay, Grandma." Joy bubbles in Katie's voice. "Hurry up and come."

I sense her infectious smile as I shout into the phone, "I'm coming... I'm coming!"

And my heart suddenly swells with feelings I had thought long dead. Tears slowly find their way down into my soul and wash away the last shreds of anger and hate; only warmth, love, and laughter remain. I close my eyes, just for a moment, and whisper, "Thank you, God."

My Prayer

Thank you for creating a heart of love inside me for my grandchildren. Even when I am feeling weary, their loving innocence fills my soul and brings me comfort.

Amen.

Unspeakable Pain

By Carrie O'Maley

Two are better than one, because they have a good return for their labor: If either of them falls down, one can help the other up. But pity anyone who falls and has no one to help them up.
~Ecclesiastes 4:9-10

I had lost my faith in God after a year of disappointments. I lost my best friend and the future I had dreamed of for as long as I could remember in a devastating breakup, and then I lost two nieces. When I thought I could not sink any lower into my grief, I fell into a debilitating depression—one so bad that I found myself unable to get out of bed to face a world that seemed to have turned against me. I felt hopeless, as though my life would only get worse, as if I were not worthy of living a happy existence.

Many of my friends had fallen away, as a listless friend is not a fun companion, nor is it easy to try to break through a stubborn shell of despair. My friend Amy, however, did not turn away. Instead, she reached out in the best way she knew how—through the presence of God.

I had not been to church in many years, and I had stopped speaking to God, feeling as though He had lost my number. But on the first Sunday of the new calendar year, Amy convinced me to attend church with her. She sat next to me in a balcony pew, singing the beautiful opening songs, and then listening attentively to the sermon. When the pastor said, "I know some of you have experienced unspeakable pain in the previous year, and you are looking for hope, looking for God to lead you through a better year," Amy squeezed my hand. In that short, simple squeeze of the hand, I felt God's presence in my relationship with Amy.

It's not always easy to see God in our everyday lives, but sometimes God makes His presence known through the caring acts of friends. I am forever indebted to Amy for re-introducing me to a God who stands beside me through the ups and downs, and reminds me to keep my faith and hope.

My Prayer

Dear God, please give me the strength to live my life with faith, hope, and love, and to stay out of despair. Keep those who love me close by to remind me of your presence in all I do.

Amen.

69

His Infinite Wisdom

By Aura Imbarus, Ph.D.

I love those who love me, and those who seek me find me.
~Proverbs 8:17

As a child, I never knew what I was praying for, nor did I truly understand the power of prayer. The idea of an omniscient God who saw everything and everybody was a conundrum to my young mind. I would always start my prayers with, "God, please help my mom, my dad, my *buni*, my grandpa, Ben—my humongous Saint Bernard—and P., my canary." Not being completely mature in my faith, I never knew if my prayers were received—or answered, for that matter. Nevertheless, through the years, I learned to trust in the mystery that was God. It was only as an adult that I was finally tested and got a new perspective on my willingness to lay my trust at God's feet.

At exactly 6:00 P.M. on December 31, 2008, my world collapsed. My mother passed away after a six-month fight with liver cancer. In that moment, upon hearing that she had taken her final breath, my brain froze, and my heart raced like never before. I was engulfed in darkness. Rica, my mom—who had been my every reason to live, breathe, and love—was gone. I couldn't fathom it. She had been the moon and the stars, the dawn and the dusk, the end and the beginning to all my days. She had been my mentor, my friend, my confidante — my everything. That life could go on without her was impossible to imagine. I had always pictured myself next to her through all of life's journeys, together forever in sickness and in health.

How could the same God to whom I had always prayed for all I needed and wanted in life take what I loved most? He lost my trust in that moment. My rage was deep and bitter. I would shed no tears; I would not dress in the traditional black; I would not mourn. I refused to make the sign of the cross again. I would not praise His name.

Tormented nights followed, one after another. One bleak night, as I lay balled up on the floor, racked by uncontrollable sobs, I found myself crying out to the emptiness despite my resolve to turn from Him. I called upon God to give me a sign that my beloved mother was all right. "Please, just one sign, that's all," I cried. "I beseech you, dear Lord. Just one sign, a small sign. Please allow me an answer."

I didn't expect a response. After all, I had turned away from Him, refused to acknowledge Him any longer. But He did hear me. Perhaps mourning my loss as much as I was, and loving me as only God can, in His infinite wisdom, He showed me His love.

In the dark room, the only light was emanating from the electronic picture frame where I was scrolling through hundreds of photos of my mother. It suddenly went blank. It turned off. No matter how much I tried to restart it: nothing. And in that sudden darkness and stillness, a peaceful wave of serenity washed through me, and I felt like I could touch infinity. I felt God put His hand on my heart.

And so it was that God had answered me — in my moments of pain, in my moments of disengaging from my faith, in my moments of railing against Him — as if to say, "She is with me; take comfort and peace in knowing this."

I could go forward.

My Prayer

Thank you, God, for never leaving us when we lose our way. Sometimes, our burdens are too overwhelming, and we find that we can no longer pray. Through you, I know I have the strength to endure whatever pain I may experience.

Amen.

Give Me Your Anger

By Kim Stokely

For men are not cast off by the Lord forever. Though he brings grief,
he will show compassion, so great is his unfailing love.
~Lamentations 3:31-32

"Where is it?" I cried as I searched the dirty car floor for what seemed like the hundredth time. Tears blurred my vision. It was hopeless. The ring was gone. The thought stabbed through me, adding new pain to my already wounded heart.

My husband had bought me the blue topaz ring as a memorial for the baby we'd lost just three weeks prior. I'd gone in for an ultrasound only to be told that my baby had died. As I was four months along, the doctor admitted me to the hospital so I could deliver my little girl. I had her on December fourth. Her birthstone would have been the topaz.

Now the ring was missing. I called the store where I'd been trying on clothes, but they hadn't found it. I searched my mother's house where I had visited after the holidays. Nothing.

My heart broke. I'd tried so hard to keep myself from giving in to my grief. After all, I had a two-year-old son who needed me. Well-meaning friends told me that obviously something had been wrong with my baby, so it was better that she died before she was born.

Others consoled me with the reminder that since I already had one child, I should have no problem getting pregnant again.

But I didn't want another baby. I wanted the baby I'd lost.

While my little boy slept on the ride back to our house, I finally had a heart-to-heart talk with God. Tired of keeping my emotions in check, I pounded the steering wheel and cried out to Him. "Why? Why did this happen? What did I do? Why do you hate me?" All my life, I'd thought it was a sin to be angry at God, but now I couldn't stop myself from yelling at Him. "You took my baby! And now you took the one thing I had to remember her by! Why are you so cruel?"

As soon as I said the words, my soul felt lighter. I could breathe easier. In that moment, God spoke to my heart. "Yes! Give me your anger. Give me your pain. It's all right. I'm big enough to handle it. And now that you've admitted it, we can work together to heal you."

We arrived home an hour later, and as I brought my son into the house, a thought shot into my mind: "Check the floor of the car." The thought continued to buzz in my brain like a fly. "Look in the car!" Finally, I went back out into the garage, got on my knees, and scrutinized the floor. "Look under the seat!" I'd searched under every seat while I was at my mother's house, but I looked again.

And there, halfway under the driver's seat, lay the ring. Slipping it on my finger, I felt God's peace. Now that I had confessed my anger, He would be faithful to bring me healing.

My Prayer

*Thank you, Lord, that in your mercy you allow us
to express all our anger and doubts without fear.
Thank you for your grace, which fills our grieving
hearts and gives us peace.*

Amen.

Chapter
8

*Devotional Stories
for*
Tough Times

Answered Prayers

*I lift up my eyes to the mountains—where does my help come from?
My help comes from the LORD, the Maker of heaven and earth.*

~Psalm 121:1-2

Walk to Jericho

By Pamela Gilsenan

By faith the walls of Jericho fell,
after the army had marched around them for seven days.
~Hebrews 11:30

Times were tight economically. All the doors were closed to jobs. Housing was expensive and sparse. Every morning after sun-up, I walked the city blocks near my house. "God, I need a job now," I prayed. "God, can't you hear me?"

I lived in a tiny, run-down former drug house close to the center of town. It took the landlord months to get the drug paraphernalia out of the basement, even though he had promised to clean before I moved in. The water in the kitchen sink didn't work for six weeks. But I didn't have a job, so I couldn't look for another place. I could barely pay for what I had. I didn't even ask God for another place, just a job. I was desperate.

Early every morning, walking in sweats, I checked businesses on my route for an indication they might need an employee. And every morning I would go home discouraged. Then I would get dressed like I was going to work and visit the unemployment office and the library to check job postings and Internet job sites.

One morning after my prayer walk, I laughed out loud, reminding God that the Israelites only had to circle Jericho for seven days before the walls came down (Joshua 6:1-20). I had been walking for weeks, but there had been no breakthrough.

The next morning, I walked past the Plains Café, the only business even open that early in the morning. There was a tattered sign in the window: "Waitress Wanted." I knew it hadn't been there the day before. I broke into a run, taking a shortcut home though the alleys. I jumped into more appropriate clothes, slapped on some make-up, and combed my hair. I was still huffing as I went back out the door. I walked slowly to the café, trying to remember my references and former job experiences for the application I anticipated filing out. I was scared even though I had decades of experience.

"Well, God," I prayed, "Jericho was a much bigger deal. This is just a hole-in-the-wall job, so you don't have to bring down a whole city. Just take care of me, please."

I got to the café, opened the door, reached for the sign in the window, and carried it to the owner. "I would like this job," I told him, handing him his sign.

"Have you any restaurant experience?" he asked.

"Line cook, prep cook, catering, prep chef, server, hostess, dish room, bus girl, school lunch lady, and restaurant assistant manager." I took a long breath.

"No one has ever handed me my sign before," he said slowly in response. "Be here tomorrow at 7:00 A.M. You can work three days a week."

The boss didn't ask for references or paperwork till several months later. By then, God had also found me a better place to live. But that is another story entirely....

My Prayer

Lord, the Bible is filled with stories of miracles
and answered prayers. I thank you for adding my
own life to this extensive list. Help me remember
that you are the one who truly knows my life's
plan and purpose.

Amen.

"Trust me, I've got the best
reference for this job...
God sent me!"

Reprinted by permission of
Stephanie Piro ©2011.

When All Doors Close

By Janet Perez Eckles

*Your ways, God, are holy. What god is as great as our God? You are the God
who performs miracles; you display your power among the peoples.*
~Psalm 77:13-14

Dead ends. Impossibilities. Closed doors. All applied to me in my sorry situation.

At age thirty-one, a retinal disease robbed my eyesight completely. The adjustment was painful. The struggle to navigate was difficult, and restoring my confidence was slow. But determination replaced the lack of confidence. I was passionate about caring for my three-, five- and seven-year-old sons. Groping through each step to perform household chores, I moved forward.

Sometimes, while at home alone, I fought negative thoughts: What kind of work does a blind person do anyway? Who would give me a job? Those were my secret concerns. I hid my feelings of worthlessness from all those around me.

"Did you ever think of becoming a Spanish interpreter?" a friend asked me one day.

"No way," I said. "I know nothing about interpreting."

"You speak Spanish," she said, "and that's a good beginning."

I contacted an interpretation company, and they asked me to come in for an oral test.

The secretary called the next day. "You passed," she said. "In fact, we're going to send you to your first assignment in the Naturalization and Immigration court tomorrow."

I gave a soft gasp. Thrilled and eager to work, I put on my business suit, grabbed my white cane, and held my husband's arm. But while waiting outside the courtroom, doubts ricocheted through my head. I knew nothing about interpretation or court proceedings.

"God, don't let me fall. Guide my steps," I prayed.

With my stomach churning, I began the session by interpreting all I heard in English into Spanish and vice versa.

The judge hit the gavel. "We'll take a ten-minute recess," he said. "Mrs. Eckles, approach the bench."

My hands trembled as I gripped my white cane and headed toward his voice.

"Yes, your Honor," I muttered.

"I'm bilingual," he said, "and I want you to know that I'm impressed with your high level of accuracy and professionalism."

I suppressed a shout of glee and smiled. "Thank you, your Honor."

Soon after, I began an intense study of audio materials on court interpretation. To my delight, I received frequent requests to interpret in civil and criminal courts. Months later, the largest over-the-phone interpreting company in America hired me because of my court experience. Through the years, I received awards for my performance, including the highest and prestigious award of Professional Excellence.

I had viewed myself as worthless; God restored my worth. I saw closed doors; God opened them wide. I lacked the skills, but He provided what I needed. I doubted the outcome, but He showed me the way.

My Prayer

Father, thank you for seeing beyond my impairment, beyond my limitations, and beyond all of what I thought were impossibilities. I thank you for seeing no one as worthless, blind, deaf or lame. You work wonders through us all!

Amen.

73

Chicken Soup
for the Soul®

Angels for All

By Lynne Graham-Orlando

*For he will command his angels concerning you
to guard you in all your ways.*
~Psalm 91:11

The phone rang at around ten o'clock on a Friday night. Our nineteen-year-old daughter, Rachel, was on the other end. "Mom, my car just died... and I don't know what to do." She was trying to catch her breath between words. I could hear the alarm in her voice.

She had left earlier that day from our home in Michigan and was headed to Florida to attend college.

"Where are you?" I asked, fighting the panic trying to creep its way in.

"I'm somewhere in Kentucky... just off I-75. My car practically died on the off-ramp, and two guys helped me push it into this parking lot." Just then a new set of thoughts crept into my mind, none of them good. Oh, Lord, help us please.

"Are they still there?"

"No, they left." Great, I thought, no help. Yet the thought of two strange men alone with our daughter wasn't exactly comforting either. Our "little girl" was stranded in the dark in a strange place hundreds of miles away. It was a very helpless feeling. She informed us that she was able to get the car started again, but it was running really rough.

By this time, my husband was pacing the floor. He was ready to jump in the car right then and there.

I told her to look around and see if there was anyone in the vicinity. She told me there was a girl at a car wash nearby. "Great. Go to the girl and ask if there is a hotel close by, maybe one you could walk to." She said that she would do that and call us back.

After we hung up, I told my husband that we needed to pray. We thanked God for sending our daughter angels to protect her in her time of need. We were both scared, but continued to pray in faith, believing God would answer our prayers. We held on to His promises.

The phone rang about five minutes later, and the relief in our daughter's voice was evident. "Oh, my gosh, Mom, she is so nice! Her name is Nicole, and she told me that I could crash at her apartment tonight. And that's not all. You won't believe it, Mom. She called her dad, and he is the manager of a muffler shop! He said that I can drop the car off tonight, and he will open up early tomorrow and fix it!"

God had exceedingly answered all our prayers!

Our daughter spent the next few days with her "angel" Nicole and her family. It was a tragic time for them because Nicole's mother had died only three days before. As our daughter helped with the mother's belongings, Nicole's aunt told her that she was their answer to prayer—their "angel."

My Prayer

*Father God, thank you for placing a ring of
protection around my children.
Continue to send your loving angels to them
during their times of need.*

Amen.

Today, Not Tomorrow

By Cari Weber

I call on you, my God, for you will answer me;
turn your ear to me and hear my prayer.
~Psalm 17:6

"I'm sorry," the bank teller said. "Your check has bounced."

Her words took a moment to sink in. This year had brought so much pain. A divorce, losing my house because of the divorce, then the loss of my job right before the holidays... and now the check for my car insurance had bounced!

Choking back tears, I asked, "May I talk with someone about the overdraft fees?"

"You can try, but my supervisor never budges."

Moments later, I met with the supervisor. I could barely explain how I recently lost my job before the tears started flowing. Incredibly, she agreed to remove all overdraft fees.

Leaving the bank, I wondered what I would do. My unemployment checks were delayed due to a glitch in the system, and everything seemed to be piling up. How long could I last without an income?

Although it was only 5:30 P.M., it was already dark outside. December in Michigan meant it was not only dark, but cold and snowy. Despite that, I had an urge to take a walk on my favorite trail.

Being cold and dark also meant there was a good chance no one else would be out, so I decided to go.

On the trail, I was grateful for sounds of rushing water coming from the creek. They covered my soft sobs while I walked. Tonight, it all felt like too much to bear.

At one point, I stopped and cried out to God. With a broken spirit, I said aloud, "Lord, I really need help right now. Today. Not tomorrow. Not the next day... today." Then I wondered: Who was I to talk to the God of the universe in this way?

Eventually, when my tears dried up, I headed home. Approaching my apartment door, I noticed something bulky hanging on the handle. Probably another bill, I thought. While I struggled with my boots, I could see a card with my name on it through the clear plastic bag. Reaching in, I took out a very small, white padded envelope. Inside the envelope was a beautiful card with no name written on it, but it was stuffed with gift cards. Hundreds of dollars of gift cards that could meet my urgent needs!

I was in shock and awe. The timing of this amazing anonymous gift, arriving at exactly the right moment, was almost too much to comprehend. Again, I began crying, but now they were tears of joy. I felt so loved. The God of the universe really cared about my little life! God heard my cries from a cold, dark, lonely place, and assured me that He does hear and will provide.

My Prayer

Father God, thank you for caring so much for us.
Knowing your love brings great hope and comfort,
especially during the darkest times. Continue to
convince us of your immeasurable love.

Amen.

75

Chicken Soup for the Soul

Help from Heaven

By Monica A. Andermann

Hear my cry for help, my King and my God, for to you I pray.
~Psalm 5:2

That morning, I awoke feeling even more overwhelmed than usual. Exhaustion had become my constant companion in the years through my mother's illness when I became caregiver to her and Dad, all while meeting the demands of a job and my own family. I hit the snooze button on my alarm clock so I could gather a few more precious moments of rest as I reviewed my day: eight hours at work, accompanying Dad to the doctor's office, returning to his home and preparing an evening meal, then finally returning to my own home for dinner, dishes, and laundry. It would be a light day by my usual standards, yet I felt I could no longer face even that schedule. I lifted my leaden feet out of bed and laid them on the floor. "God," I called out in a moment of sheer desperation, "I can't do this anymore. Please help me."

I managed to drag myself to work where I was called into the department director's office. I was informed of a department-wide layoff, given a cardboard box for my personal items, and told to pack up and leave. In the numb moments afterward, as I cleaned out my desk, I remembered my earlier plea. A simple call of help to the heavens had so often been the most effective prayer when other words had failed me. But losing my job was not exactly the answer I had expected. Somehow, though, I sensed it was. I just had to trust. So I did.

Soon, I discovered that my unexpected "vacation" had left me feeling so relaxed that I became a better caregiver to my parents. I barely worried about my stack of unpaid bills or the dead ends that greeted my job search. However, money was a real concern, and to that end, it seemed that I now required a college degree to stay competitive in my field. I had wanted a college degree for so long, but had never had the time to pursue this dream. Now I had time, but no income. I felt stuck at a crossroads between my needs and my desires, wondering why God had led me down this path only to be met with disappointment. I found myself again praying my one simple prayer: Help!

And help came again.

Within days, I discovered a college program specifically designed for adults with demanding lives like mine. I was able to garner credits from life experience and set my own schedule, which allowed me to continue caring for my family. Tuition money came from a variety of unexpected sources, too, as did funds to pay bills. Several times, I actually found money in the street—one time, a fifty-dollar bill! God had heard my prayer that desperate morning and provided fulfillment for His answer every step of the way. He forged the path, and I just went along for the ride. And what a wonderful ride it is when we trust in His plan.

My Prayer

*Father, fill me with the Holy Spirit when life's
uncertainty invades my world. Replace my
anxieties with confidence that you have not given
my anything I cannot handle. Let me find comfort
that you are always with me on this wonderful
ride of life.*

Amen.

76

Hanging On for Dear Life

By Teresa Cook

*For this reason a man will leave his father and mother
and be united to his wife, and they will become one flesh.*
~Genesis 2:24

Despite nearly twenty years of marriage, I barely recognized the man I had married. My normally kind and gentle husband was sullen and snapped at the slightest provocation. He seemed to take everything I said the wrong way. While I knew every marriage goes through periods of stress, I always thought ours would weather the storms. Now, I wasn't so sure.

One night, the hostility escalated. Angry words flew back and forth. At one point, Michael beat the bed as he spoke, accentuating each word with a punch. I had never feared my husband before that moment and silently prayed for protection. Instantly, an irrational and unspeakable calm came over me, allowing me to answer Michael in a non-threatening manner, yet still express what I needed to say.

The next morning, however, I fumed at the night's events. Though fearful the night before, I knew I was in no danger. My husband's outburst was not a pattern for him, not his typical way of responding. Rather, it was an indication of the strain Michael was under and an expression of the pain he felt because of our conflicts. Still, I was angry. The constant bickering exhausted me, and thoughts of divorce filled my mind. I was at the end of my proverbial rope.

Then God threw me a lifeline.

Michael didn't do an about-face and fervently apologize for all the things he had done to hurt me. I had no stunning revelation about why our marriage was plummeting down the tubes. God simply told me to "hang on." So I did.

I hung on through two years of marriage counseling, when we aired our grievances and reopened old wounds in front of a stranger. I hung on to the psalmist's words to "be strong and take heart and wait for the LORD" (Psalm 27:14). I hung on to the assurance that God can and does change lives. Each day, I hung on for one more day.

Gradually, things changed. A smile here, a shared laugh there. During the dark times, God sent the Holy Spirit to give me the same peace He imparted that angry night. Through prayer, He changed us each a little at a time. And all the while, I hung on.

When we married, Michael and I united as "one flesh." You can't divide one flesh and not leave lives ripped apart. So I hung on for dear life—our life together. Now, after thirty-five years of marriage, I'm so glad I did.

My Prayer

*Father, you ordained marriage as a covenant
relationship. Remind us of that when the world
tells us it's okay to just quit and move on.
Heal our wounds and bind our hearts
so we can truly become one flesh.*

Amen.

77

Surprise Letter

By Teresa Hoy

And my God will meet all your needs
according to the riches of his glory in Christ Jesus.
~Philippians 4:19

I dropped the checkbook onto the kitchen table and buried my face in my hands. I wanted to cry. No matter how I calculated and refigured, I was fifty dollars short to pay a bill that month. Where was I going to get the extra money?

Being newly married, I didn't know exactly what other accounts we had or even where they were located. I didn't have any spare money from my job or any hidden savings account to draw from. I could have asked my husband's advice, but he was on a military flying assignment and couldn't easily be reached. And I couldn't wait for his return. The bill was due in a few days.

I shoved back from the table, frowning, and began to pace. I ended up in the living room, striding back and forth, my hands clasped behind my back as I stared at the carpet. Every now and then I let out a troubled sigh. Dread wended its way through me, like a thorny vine prickling and squeezing tighter and tighter, until I could hardly breathe from worry. At that point, I did the only thing I knew to do. I dropped to my knees and prayed, "Oh, God, I know I shouldn't worry, but I can't figure out what to do. I trust that you will help me find a way to pay that bill." After that, I stopped pacing. I put away the calculator and checkbook.

A couple of days later, I got the mail and found an envelope addressed to my husband. Since my husband was gone so much, I always opened all of the mail as soon as it arrived. I opened the envelope and took out the folded sheet of paper. Something slid from inside the letter and floated to the floor. My heart somersaulted when I picked it up and saw it was a check for the exact amount of fifty dollars. I didn't recognize the name of the man who signed the letter, but he thanked my husband for lending him the money on an Air Force flight two years earlier. He was sorry it had taken him so long to pay it back.

I was suddenly crying joyful tears. The beauty of God is that He never gives me too much or too little. He gives me exactly what I need. I bowed my head and poured out my thanks.

My Prayer

God, I am humbled by how much you love me.
Please keep me mindful of all the ways you
provide for me, both great and small, and never
let me take your blessings for granted.

Amen.

Past My Expiration Date

By Shelley Mosley

But those who hope in the LORD will renew their strength.
They will soar on wings like eagles; they will run and not grow weary,
they will walk and not be faint.
~Isaiah 40:31

I sat with my husband and parents in the bleachers watching my son and daughter march proudly with their teams in the soccer parade. As I raised my arm to wave at them, pain shot from my shoulder to my fingers. A red, stinging rash covered my hand. My head felt as though it would explode at any moment, and I was so dizzy I needed to lie down. Fortunately, the parade came to an end, and I could go home and rest.

I tried to stand, but I couldn't move. Somehow, my family got me down the bleachers and into the car. I was exhausted. As soon as I got home, I fell into bed. After I awoke, I glanced at a mirror. My face was swollen, and a red rash covered the bridge of my nose, part of my cheeks and my forehead.

Two days later, I told the doctor about my experience at the soccer parade. "Shelley," he said gently, "I'm afraid you have lupus." He arranged for me to see a rheumatologist as soon as possible.

I called my husband and mother. Although they were upset, I had an odd sense of peace. For several years, my random symptoms had been severe enough to send me to the doctor. They had tested me for everything, including lupus, but the tests always came back negative. Putting a label on what was wrong with me made it easier. Now my enemy had a name. With God's help, I could fight it.

A few days later, I saw the rheumatologist. This time, my tests came back positive and verified the other doctor's diagnosis. We discussed my treatment and changes I needed to make to my lifestyle. Then he dropped the bomb. He said if I took my medications, got plenty of rest, stayed out of the sun, and got a check-up every three months, I might live as long as ten years... if I was lucky. Ten years sounds like a lot of time, but I had a six-year-old daughter and a nine-year-old son, and it was possible I wouldn't live another year, let alone ten. Even in the best case, I wouldn't be around to see Jessica graduate from high school.

The doctor tried various combinations of medications on me. Some of them made me feel so much sicker that I didn't think I'd make the one-year mark. I joined a lupus support group, but their death rate was high. I dropped out, determined not to join their numbers. As the years went on, I developed more autoimmune problems—fibromyalgia, arthritis, and Sjogren's syndrome—but I kept going.

I asked God for one thing over and over—to let me live long enough to raise my children. He has answered my prayer with abundance. I made it to my ten-year deadline. The years went by. By His grace, I'm fourteen years past what my husband calls "my expiration date."

I will always believe in miracles. After all, I'm living one.

My Prayer

Dear Lord, you bless us with your miracles,
but too often we don't recognize them for what
they are. Help us to see and be thankful
for your many gifts.

Amen.

79

Ask, Receive, Thank

By Arlene Rains Graber

"If you believe, you will receive whatever you ask for in prayer."
~Matthew 21:22

I stared at the letter. The return address blazed in huge bold letters. IRS. A frown spread across my face, and I could feel my blood pressure rise. I tore it open. Without reading the commentary, I went right to the bottom line. Past Due.

Great. Mr. Tax Man, get in line. There are a slew of bills ahead of you. Utilities. Mortgage. Credit card.

It had been a tough year. While the economy slid south, my freelance writing business joined, producing rejection after rejection. Periodicals were cutting back. Some were even shutting down. Newspapers were overworking staff instead of hiring correspondents. I sighed and looked out the kitchen window to check on Palmer, my four-year-old grandson. Oh, to have his innocence and world without stress.

In a fury, I began cleaning the kitchen. I was deep in soap suds when Palmer bounded into the house. "Nana, can I have an ice cream bar?"

"Sure," I answered, reaching into the freezer.

He expressed little surprise, but his broad smile and twinkling eyes spoke volumes. "Thanks."

He asked, received, and thanked the giver. I grinned, remembering that I, too, had someone larger and generous: God. Right then and there, I prayed for guidance toward economic relief, and a huge weight lifted from my shoulders. I'd given the problem to someone else. It was going to be okay.

The weeks whizzed by. Nothing. Although in my heart I knew that God would take care of me, I sure wished He'd hurry! Then, just as I was about to take a menial part-time job, I received a phone call.

"Would you be interested in writing an article for us this month?"

It was a national magazine, and the pay was more than adequate to cover the taxes. I was relieved, thinking the assignment couldn't have come at a better time. A few days later, I opened what I assumed was yet another rejection from a publisher. My eyes widened in surprise as I read an acceptance followed by a W-2 form. Even though I'd prayed about this particular submission, which was a difficult article to unravel, I was proud, crediting my good work instead of thanking the person who guided my pen.

The good news kept coming. An old investment that lay dormant suddenly sprang to life, producing additional income. I was dancing all over the kitchen, elated at my windfall, when Palmer called.

"Nana, can I come over and play in your backyard?"

"Sure. Tell your mother I'll be right over to get you."

I hung up, and it hit me. Ask, receive, thank. My eyes scanned the assignment on my desk and a check nearby. Good work? Maybe, but without God there would have been no resolution to my financial woes. A simple lesson from a four-year-old boy.

My Prayer

Lord, thank you for answering my prayers in your divine time. Even when the answers are to slow to appear, help me to remain humble and remember that I am nothing without you.

Amen.

80

The Envelope

By Kathryn Lay

He replied, "Because you have so little faith. Truly I tell you,
if you have faith as small as a mustard seed, you can say to this mountain,
'Move from here to there,' and it will move.
Nothing will be impossible for you."
~Matthew 17:20

My dream of motherhood seemed to be disappearing. After the tenth negative pregnancy test in less than five years, I had given up hope of ever being called "Mom." My husband and I were surrounded by pregnant family and friends. We loved them all, but it was a constant reminder of the loss we were feeling.

"Don't you love us anymore?" I asked God one morning. "I don't understand why I'm not pregnant yet." The pain seemed more than I could bear.

One afternoon, a friend came by my house. We'd known each other since college, and I knew she cared about my pain.

"I believe God will answer your prayers in an amazing way," she said.

I burst into tears, wanting to believe her.

"What will your first child's name be?" she asked.

"Michael or Michelle," I answered. Richard and I had chosen the names long ago, before we married.

She wrote something on a piece of paper, folded it, and put it in an envelope. "Open this when he or she arrives."

I put the envelope in a pocket of my purse, figuring I would never have the opportunity to read what was inside.

"Have faith," she said before she left.

Five years went by, and Richard and I still longed for a child. Then, one morning, a friend called to tell us about the classes she and her husband were taking to be eligible for adoption through the state. We signed up right away.

Seven months later, we'd been approved, having completed our parenting classes, home studies, and paperwork. It was time to wait again, but this time there was hope.

And on November 2, 1992, the call came. We had been accepted for adoption of a nine-month-old girl. Her foster parents named her Michelle.

God had answered our long hours of prayer. It hadn't been the way I'd expected, but the results were all that I had dreamed. My daughter is the joy of my life.

It wasn't until nearly a year later, cleaning out my closet, that I found an old purse. I rummaged through it as my daughter played around my feet. In a zippered pocket was an envelope. I opened it and found a mustard seed necklace and a folded piece of paper. I read the note my friend had written. "Kathy, give little Michael or Michelle a hug for me. Never give up faith or hope."

I glanced down at Michelle and smiled. She grinned back. "Mama."

My friend had planted seeds of faith in my heart. God had watered them, and my dream came to life and called me Mama.

My Prayer

When it seems that all hope is lost, let me
remember the sweet and simple words,
"God is with me." I thank you for bringing people
into my life who help strengthen my faith when it
rests on rocky soil. You are the one true Father!
In your name…

Amen.

81

Chicken Soup for the Soul

Still Looking After Me

By Katie A. Mitchell

"Look at the birds of the air; they do not sow or reap or store away in barns,
and yet your Heavenly Father feeds them.
Are you not much more valuable than they?"
~Matthew 6:26

I did the final calculation on my monthly bills and matched the total against the checkbook balance. Short again. I needed another $169.90 to be caught up with the month's expenses. Where was I going to get $169.90? It simply wasn't in the bank or in my wallet. I put down the pencil, leaned back, and thought again of Daddy.

It had been just six weeks since he passed away. Even after he had gone into the nursing home a year and a half earlier, he still worried about me and often asked if I had enough money. He was most concerned about being able to help and being a supportive daddy. I kept telling him he would always be a daddy to me no matter what and to not worry about me. But, somehow, when I needed extra money and without ever telling him, he would slip some in my hand and smile.

With a heavy heart, I got up from the table and wandered over to the kitchen. I picked up the phone and reviewed the calls I had missed. One name and number came up two or three times. Who was this guy? On a whim, I called the number, and an unfamiliar male voice answered. I told him who I was, explained that his name and number had appeared on my Caller ID, and asked how I could help him.

He explained that he had periodically bought copies of a folklore book my dad had written directly from him, but he had run out. When he called the nursing home, they told him that Daddy had passed away and gave him my phone number.

"Do you still have those books available?" he asked. I told him I still had a few in my possession.

"Well, I would like to purchase twenty-four of them," he said. "He normally sold them to me at $6 apiece, but I'm thinking that since you're almost out of them, maybe you should charge more. I would be willing to pay $7 a copy."

We made arrangements for him to pick up the books, and then I hung up the phone and did a quick calculation of twenty-four books at $7 apiece. Choking back tears, I stared at the total. It came to $168—just a dollar and ninety cents short of what I needed to meet the rest of my monthly bills.

Daddy was still looking out for me.

My Prayer

Dear Lord, thank you so much for the precious love of our fathers who support, encourage, and care about our daily needs. Allow us to remember that, as much as they love us, how much more you, our Heavenly Father, will be there to love and care for us throughout eternity if we but come to you with all our cares and burdens.

Amen.

Chapter
9

Devotional Stories for Tough Times

Truth in the Word

For I am the LORD your God who takes hold of your right hand and says to you, Do not fear; I will help you.

~Isaiah 41:13

82

Finding God in a Dumpster

By Corinne A. Hummel

He said to his disciples, "Why are you so afraid? Do you still have no faith?"
~Mark 4:40

Dumpster diving is an honorable occupation. Rescuing cans from the town Dumpsters and seeing them safely to the local recycle center provides the aluminum with a future and me with much-needed cash. My life as a certified nurse's aide had come to an abrupt end when safety restraints were declared harsh restrictions of patient rights. Mattresses were placed on the floor to prevent patient falls. Nurse's aides then had to work by kneeling on the floor and using terrible body mechanics to do patient care. My beat-up, battered, old body let me know my working days were over, and a doctor declared me 100 percent disabled.

Disabled! Self-respect took a major dive. Independence? Ha! My lifetime motto, "I can take care of myself—with God's help," became "With God's help, I can survive." Food stamps and money for rent came from the state. Nutritious, healthy food became a luxury, and extras evaporated.

I discovered Dumpster diving after town officials voted to end curbside trash collection. Three industrial-size Dumpsters appeared, and people adjusted to dumping stuff in a central place. Locals didn't throw away much good stuff, but keen observation and desperation showed me a prime time for Dumpster diving. The local lake hosted a weekend population from the nearby big city. On Sunday evening, city folks would pack up and head home, stopping at the Dumpsters with their trash. Bingo! When the parade of cars leaving town rolled away, my trusty grabber and I got busy.

Standing on my sturdy, three-step ladder, I used my grabber to pull a box toward me. It was full of cans, and I was counting the money as I reached for it. That's when I spotted the book—well, half a book. I parked the box of cans on my Radio Flyer to retrieve it. A Bible! Well, half a Bible. I didn't know whether to laugh or cry for the person so stressed that he or she tore the book in two. So I laughed with a God who would let me know I was in His sights even while Dumpster diving.

That's when I focused on the top page of the halved Bible. Past the crumpled creases, I read Mark 4:40, "'Why are you so afraid? Do you still have no faith?'" I sat down on my ladder and cried. All the prayers, all the struggles, all the survival techniques came into focus: With God at my side, who can win against me? He used a Dumpster dive to remind me that He is ever with me, and I can never drift beyond His everlasting arms. I wiped away my tears, looked up with heartfelt thanks, and went digging for the other half of the Bible. Reunited, the two halves live in the glove compartment of my pick-up truck where His words remind me of His presence—all the time.

My Prayer

*God, I pray for the lost souls who throw away
your Word. May all who feel disconnected and
lost right now open their hearts and allow you to
enter. Help them to see that you always offer hope
and a solution to their pain.*

Amen.

83

Resurrection Faith

By Sally Clark

I will give them a heart to know me, that I am the LORD.
~Jeremiah 24:7

"W e've got to go. Now!" My husband leaned over the choir rail and whispered insistently.

"Why? The service just started," I asked in hushed tones.

"Now! There's been an accident."

As our twenty-year-old son and his eighteen-year-old fiancée were driving to church that Sunday, their car flipped over, and they were both injured. The hospital would not give any details, saying only that we should come right away.

A doctor met us at the door and asked all of us to follow him into a room down the hall. That's where he told us that Krista was dead, her body thrown out the passenger's side open window and crushed when the car rolled over on her. Doug's injuries were not serious.

My heart kept saying this could not be true, but my head told me that it was. What's more, my head was telling me that God was real. Totally real. God was more real to me in that moment than the flesh hanging from my son's ribs. God was real. There was no more doubt.

In the weeks that followed, my tears came as easily as breathing.

My husband, my son, Krista's family—we all suffered more than we thought we could stand. It drove me to my knees for the first time in my life.

"What do I do, Lord? How can we get through this?" I pleaded. The answer I received silenced me.

"I want you to know me. I want you to know who I am."

I don't think I actually expected God to answer me, but this was certainly not anything I had imagined I would hear. These were not my words or my thoughts. I knew that much. I had heard God's voice inside my own heart for the first time, and I knew He was inviting me to know Him in ways that I had never known Him before. But how, I wondered, was I supposed to know God better? Through the Bible.

So I began to read. I devoured the Word like a starving woman at a banquet. The more I ate, the hungrier I was. And the closer I got to God, the harder my life situations became. Things got worse, much worse, before they got better, but slowly, we healed. Over time, I came to understand that though circumstances are painful, I have no control over what God will do, only faith that He is good. And I live with the humility of knowing that my faith came to life through Krista's dying, for somewhere in her death, I found the words of resurrection.

My Prayer

*Father, you are real and you are everywhere, even
in death. Thank you that my life in you can never
die or stop or end for I am always in your hands.*

Amen.

The New Teacher

By Dorothy K. LaMantia

"For this is what the LORD, the God of Israel, says: 'The jar of flour will not be used up and the jug of oil will not run dry until the day the LORD sends rain on the land.'" She went away and did as Elijah had told her. So there was food every day for Elijah and for the woman and her family.
~1 Kings 17:14-15

"You look like you've had a toothache for the last six weeks," said Nancy. "Are you okay?"

"Oh, sure. I'm just tired," I lied, unwilling to admit to a co-worker that my becoming a teacher was a mistake and that I doubted I would last that first year. Making it to November looked uncertain.

During the job interview, I impressed the principal and the English supervisor with confidence and enthusiasm—even when they explained that the students assigned to me would be difficult, and the program lacked a curriculum and books. The supervisor promised, "Don't worry. I'll mentor you. We'll work together."

On the eve of my first day, my mentor handed me a box of discarded books and said, "You might find something useful here." She paused, and then blurted, "Dorothy, I'm sorry. I've accepted another job. I won't be here to help you." She headed to her office to pack, leaving me stunned, though unshaken.

But Day One shook me. Teachers say the first weeks are easy, with students eager to make a good impression. My students' glazed eyes, sullen faces, and rude responses hinted we would have no honeymoon. Still, I believed my upbeat attitude would carry me. But it held no sway over kids biding their time until they could quit school forever. I shopped for motivational strategies and educated myself on teaching at-risk children. But the struggles only escalated. Within two weeks, a lump in my throat and a tightness in my gut were constant.

One Sunday, I was scheduled to read the Scripture passages at church. When I opened my Bible to rehearse, I found the assigned verses in Chapter 17 of the Book of Kings. The widow of Zarephath, expecting that she and her son would die of starvation, received this promise from the prophet Elijah: "The jar of flour will not be used up and the jug of oil will not run dry..." The knot in my stomach loosened at the words, "So there was food every day for Elijah and for the woman and her family." In those words, I detected a sign that translated into "Don't worry. You'll make it until June."

At school, the kids and the job did not change that much. But I did, as I claimed God's promise and faced each day with strength and confidence. Nancy even noticed that I was smiling again. Several weeks later, the principal stopped to say, "I am impressed. Yesterday, I stood outside your door. I never saw a teacher get as much out of those kids as you did."

"Thank you, sir," I answered. But to the One who is truly in charge, I prayed, "Thank you, God, for the graces to recognize that I only have the power to change myself and to know that with your help I can meet any challenge life sets before me."

My Prayer

Lord, help me be mindful that the little things
I do every day when I am teaching others, I do
for you. Thank you for allowing me to fulfill my
spiritual gift of teaching and to become a better
Christian in the process.

Amen.

85

All Things Work Together

By Linda A. Haywood

And we know that in all things God works for the good of those who love him,
who have been called according to his purpose.
~Romans 8:28

On December 22, 2008, I arrived to work at my usual time and began my day by reading my e-mails. One e-mail in particular caught my attention. It was from my supervisor, and it read, "I have scheduled a meeting with you at 4:45 P.M. today. If you have already scheduled visits for this time, please reschedule those visits."

All that day I walked around feeling as though I was in limbo. Something just didn't feel quite right. Questions flooded my mind. "Why are my co-workers avoiding me? Why would my supervisor schedule a meeting with me fifteen minutes before the end of the day? Why? Why? Why?"

At the meeting, my supervisor and one of her peers sat across from me as she launched into a discussion regarding my position. Then she casually ended by saying, "And therefore the agency has decided to let you go." As her words echoed in my ears, I felt like a trapeze artist who had flown mid-air and let go of the bars, only to discover that there was no one there to catch me. I imagined myself falling, futilely flailing and screaming, with only three days before Christmas, one work check in my checking account, and six months short of having the ability to obtain the pension that I would have received from the agency as a vested employee.

Despite the media reports of the many unemployed who were losing their homes, I did marvelously the first month of unemployment. I loudly proclaimed that my job was not my god, and just like He blessed me with that job, God would open another door for me. I held on to every scripture in the Bible that spoke of God's faithfulness, chiefly, "… in all things God works for the good of those who love him…"

By the second month of my unemployment, I had run out of money and was two months behind on my rent and car payments. At that point, my fears kicked in and tried to weigh me down with visions of joblessness, homelessness, and no vehicle to escape the winter cold and snow. Many days I held on to God's promises to comfort my distress as I prayed for rescue.

Just as my hopes began to fade, God's faithfulness materialized right before my eyes, and my situation turned around to the good. First, instead of evicting me, my landlord said, "Linda, I'll work with you on this. Just keep me posted as to how things are going." Second, the company that finances my car also agreed to work with me and didn't repossess my car. Finally, I received a call from a temp service that had reviewed my resume online. I ended up being hired for a job where I'm still doing what I love and currently making over $10,000 more per year than I was making at my previous place of employment. God is good.

My Prayer

Dear Father God, thank you for your faithfulness toward us and how you are always working things out on our behalf. Thank you for your presence as we go through every one of our trials and tribulations, and for giving us the reassurance that you indeed are with us always, even unto the end of the world.

Amen.

86

Listening to Him

By Robbie Iobst

Blessed are those whose strength is in you,
whose hearts are set on pilgrimage.
~Psalm 84:5

On a Wednesday night eight years ago, I discovered my husband's lies and left him. The note I put on his chair in the living room told him I just couldn't live with him anymore. It was all over.

I needed to be alone to think and pray, so I took my four-year-old son to Gamma's house and went to spend the night with my friend, Desha. That night, I found myself sobbing in Desha's bathroom. Lying on her spotless bathroom floor, I held my Bible and prayed, "God, I need to hear you clearly."

I opened my Bible, and my eyes settled on Psalm 84:5: "Blessed are those... whose hearts are set on pilgrimage."

God revealed Himself to me, comforted me, and told me the truth through His Word. Blessed are those who have hearts set on pilgrimage. The ones who persevere through the journey are the ones who live in blessing. In that moment, I knew I needed to persevere in my marriage.

At first, I said, "No!" I wasn't the one who had lied. I wasn't the one who had betrayed the trust in our marriage. But as I continued to cry and pray, God showed me that I had done things that hurt our marriage. I wasn't blameless.

A week later, my son and I returned home. John and I entered counseling and began the long road, the long pilgrimage, to putting our marriage back together. God walked with us each step of the way.

Seven months later, we stood on the beach, surrounded by close friends, and renewed our vows. Our marriage was restored because God told us, through the Bible and His people, to hang in there even when we felt like running. It wasn't easy, but it was worth it. At the top of our invitation to the renewal of our vows, we placed Psalm 84:5. And then we wrote: Blessed is the couple whose heart is set on marriage.

My Prayer

Father, thank you for your guidance in our daily lives. We are so fortunate that your love shines upon us even when we are filled with despair. May we always be open to your healing touch in our lives and relationships.

Amen.

87

I Have Overcome!

By Brenda Redmond

"The LORD who rescued me from the paw of the lion and the paw of the bear will rescue me from the hand of this Philistine." Saul said to David, "Go, and the LORD be with you."
~1 Samuel 17:37

I struggled to catch my breath. I felt like I was drowning. My grief consumed me. Like a flood, the waves of sadness seemed to wash over me. I sat on my couch feeling drained and alone. What were we going to do?

Life had taken a sudden turn. It was without warning, as most disasters are. One day, everything was fine, and then the next...

My husband and I had both lost our jobs. Financially, we were in trouble. Deep, deep trouble. We had tried to struggle through and make minimum payments, but there was no use. How were we going to pay our bills, let alone put food on the table?

I watched my two-year-old daughter play on the floor with her dolls, totally unaware of how our lives were falling apart. She had been our miracle baby. We had waited a long time for her. We needed another miracle right now. New tears overtook me.

I reached for my Bible, desperately needing the Lord to comfort me, to somehow show me that everything would be okay. I opened the pages to the story of David and Goliath.

"'The LORD who rescued me from the paw of the lion and the paw of the bear will rescue me from the hand of this Philistine.'"

All of a sudden, it dawned on me. I had overcome things, too. Certainly not as extreme as the obstacles that David overcame, but obstacles nonetheless.

Right there in my living room, I stood up. I took a deep breath. With a renewed determination, I shouted, "I have overcome barrenness! I have overcome losing my job! I have overcome lack! The Lord will deliver us from this, too."

My daughter looked at me like I was crazy, and I laughed at her expression. Mommy wasn't crazy. All of a sudden, Mommy had received a revelation of the faithfulness of God. I knew that I was an overcomer. Just as God was faithful to be there to help David overcome his obstacles, He'd be there for me, too. It was going to be okay.

And before I knew it, all was well again. God had once again been faithful.

My Prayer

Lord, please help me to remember that I can trust
you to help me overcome obstacles in my path.
You have always been there for me before, and I
know that I can always find victory when I walk
hand in hand with you.

Amen.

The Great Physician

By Ann Holbrook

And the prayer offered in faith will make the sick person well;
the Lord will raise them up…
~James 5:15

"The test results show you have ovarian cancer."

When I heard those piercing words spoken by my gynecologist, shock and fear enveloped me. Nothing could have prepared me for the extensive exploratory surgery, the four-hour-long chemotherapy treatments over the next several months, or the resulting weakness, hair loss, and extreme stress. Why did this deadly disease attack my body? The question haunted me nearly every day.

According to the surgeon, my prognosis for surviving Stage III(C) ovarian cancer was only 8-13 percent for the next five years. I felt God had abandoned me. Tentacles of palpable loneliness wrapped around my heart. I didn't know of any women who had been stricken with ovarian cancer and lived through it. There were no examples to follow, no hope to be garnered from other humans. Tears were cried in vain... or so it seemed.

In desperation, I turned to the Bible for solace. As I read more and more Scriptures about the love and compassion Jesus demonstrated to those He met, my broken heart slowly began to mend. The account in the New Testament gospels of the woman with horrendous female problems resonated with me. Her hope in Jesus ignited faith, and healing came by simply touching the hem of His garment. If Christ cared enough to stop in His tracks, turn, and tell this woman her faith had made her well, maybe I could believe for my healing, too.

Word of my illness spread quickly among family and friends, and the ripple effect became huge. Prayers from people all over the country were lifted on my behalf.

As I healed emotionally, my body also began to be restored. When each blood test came back from the lab with excellent results, I felt a flood of relief and increased hope.

Finally, after a tough year, I was pronounced cancer-free. A total miracle.

This occurred fifteen years ago. Like the woman in the gospels, I believe my illness and suffering made me reach out to the Great Physician—the only one who could understand as well as triumph over all obstacles.

Cancer forced me to stop and consider what is really important. I do not take my health or anyone else's for granted. I've learned to cherish my relationships with my Creator, family, and friends. These are far more important than the busyness of this life.

My Prayer

Father, I pray for those who have lost hope because of their suffering. I ask that you would ignite the flame of faith and empower them to trust in you. In Jesus's name…

Amen.

Promises for the Jobless

By Nancy B. Kennedy

Jesus looked at them and said, "With man this is impossible,
but with God all things are possible."
~Matthew 19:26

Sadly, most of our friends have been laid off at one time or another. Many have had to move away to find work. We seemed the most stable family we knew. My husband grew up in the area and had worked for just two employers in twenty years. I'd lived here for twenty-five years. We'd been married for twenty years and lived in our house for fifteen.

Yet, one day, the ax fell for us, too. "They're eliminating jobs in a certain salary range," John said. "My salary range."

In that instant, my life of carefully constructed security vanished. We were stunned that John got so little in severance pay. Unemployment insurance paid just a fraction of his income. How were we going to live?

Jobless, we suffered financial shocks almost daily. Our washer broke, an air conditioner died, and our car needed repairs. Our property was reassessed, and our real estate taxes skyrocketed. My hand shook as I wrote checks and watched our bank balance plummet.

It was exhausting to shield our young son from the crest of our emotions. In my despair, I found it difficult to read the Bible or even to pray. One Sunday, our pastor prayed for those who needed jobs, and I fled the sanctuary in tears. I hated being counted among the needy ones.

It was at an almost subconscious level, then, that a verse of Scripture reached my heart. I imagine that just about every Christian has confidently said that "with God all things are possible" (Matthew 19:26). I'd said it myself, although I wasn't sure I believed it anymore.

But it was this promise that sustained us during those bleak months of joblessness. I thought of it every time we were blessed with an unexpected kindness—the neighbors who made us meals, the farm stand that refused my money, the camp director who waived our fees. We received a steady stream of cards and phone calls, soothing hugs and words of encouragement.

Most memorable, though, was the Sunday morning we entered the church classroom where my husband has taught a group of believers for years. A stack of envelopes was piled high on his chair. There, among our cherished friends, we opened the cards one by one. Each envelope contained a check. I wept as we made our way through the stack. Adding it up later, we were stunned to find that our friends had given us more than $2,000. What riches of mercy are found in the love of God's people! Once again, I can say confidently: "With God all things are possible."

My Prayer

Dear God, with you, everything is possible. You have promised to supply all my needs, because in you all richness is found. Help me to believe your promises and let me experience the joy of them as I look for work.

Amen.

90

Uncle Walt's Legacy

By Shirley Pieters Vogel

"… God is the strength of my heart and my portion forever."
~Psalm 73:26

Asking for directions to Uncle Walt's room, I wondered if he would know me and my mom. Or would he be like the confused patients grabbing at us as we walked by? Always kind and willing to help others, he was now sometimes verbally abusive. "Please, God, not to us," I prayed.

Sitting lopsided in a chair, Uncle Walt stared straight ahead. I tried to ignore his disheveled clothes. When he looked vacantly at me, I missed seeing his slightly crooked smile that always reminded me of my father. There was no apparent recognition, and I wanted Uncle Walt to remember how much we loved each other. Had Alzheimer's already stolen that?

"Uncle Walt, do you know me?" After what seemed a long time, he said, "You're my niece, uh…" Afraid he couldn't finish, I said, "Yes, I'm Shirley." Hugging him, I motioned my mother to come nearer. Kissing him, she said, "I'm your brother Milt's wife, Jennie."

Mom and I talked until, gradually, Uncle Walt delighted us with even his shortest answers. But, at times, he would slip away, leaving us with an expressionless stranger. I wanted to reach in and pull out my Uncle Walt.

As I picked up his Bible, Mom suggested I read Psalm 128, and then added, "Remember, Walt, it was your mother's favorite." I began, "Blessed are all who fear the LORD..." And Uncle Walt recited the rest—never hesitating! Smiling, he said, "I used to recite that psalm daily."

A nurse later found him on the floor next to his bed. Refusing to get up, he explained, "I'm saying my prayers." Although Uncle Walt's relationship with me was impaired, his walk with God remained solid, and his example spoke volumes. Blessed are those who fear the Lord—everyone! What a legacy!

My Prayer

Almighty God, we thank and praise you for reminding us that nothing can separate us from your love—not even Alzheimer's disease. May we always remember that you love us more than we can ever understand. Even when our loved ones' memories fade, help us find comfort in knowing that you always know them by name.

Amen.

Chapter
10

Devotional Stories for Tough Times

Count Your Blessings

The LORD has done it this very day; let us rejoice today and be glad.

~Psalm 118:24

91

The Tire Swing

By Liz Every Cook

*It was majestic in beauty, with its spreading boughs,
for its roots went down to abundant waters.*
~Ezekiel 31:7

Therapy began at an early age for me. It began right there on our farm, hanging from the old mulberry tree. It wasn't fancy and didn't cost an arm and a leg. As a matter of fact, it was absolutely free!

What made my therapy so special? Maybe it was the hundred-year-old mulberry tree that provided shade from the hot summer sun, its leaves singing a gentle song as they rustled in the breeze. The birds sang for me from its huge branches, and delicious mulberries provided snacks as well as stains on my clothes. The day my dad threw a rope over one of the biggest branches and attached an old tire was the first day of my childhood therapy.

All a tire swing needs is a child with some imagination. I climbed on top of the tire, pretending it was a horse, threaded my body through the tire on my stomach or sat in the tire as it swung back and forth. The rope holding the tire could be twisted tightly, providing a wild dizzy ride once it was released. But the very best part was simply lazily swinging back and forth, allowing my mind to drift as my body relaxed. The mesmerizing gentle motion back and forth, the whisper of a breeze, and the quiet peacefulness surrounding me were heavenly. I felt safe and happy, as if nothing bad could ever touch me there.

I found it impossible to be unhappy, mad or sad in my tire swing. I might brood a while at first, but as the swing worked its magic, I would begin to sing. My collie, Tippy, liked to position herself so that my body would brush against her as I swung. She patiently sat there with me as I sang, not seeming to mind that my voice wasn't great. She listened patiently as I spilled out my childhood problems, and between the two of us, we worked everything out. I will always remember those big brown eyes watching me as I talked, as though every word I said was totally fascinating. And she never expected anything but a pat on the head or a hug around her big, furry neck.

Those childhood days are gone, the old mulberry tree is long since dead, and the collie dog is no more. I couldn't fit my sixty-three-year-old butt into a tire swing if I had to. My problems and frustrations are not the simple ones of childhood, and my neighbors would probably report me for disturbing the peace if I attempted to sing about them. Yet I still experience the calming effects of swinging as the gentle breeze plays over my skin. Now I sit in my porch swing with comfy pillows all around me, reading a book or simply closing my eyes and listening to the sounds of nature or the children playing down the street. I talk to God, and He listens even more intently than my dog... and between the two of us, we work things out!

My Prayer

Creator God, how fortunate we are that you created trees, swings, and dogs to bring comfort to our lives. You give us places to talk intimately with you, and we find serenity in knowing that you listen to all our prayers.

Amen.

"An old tire, a tree and a dog...
I hope I'll always remember that
life doesn't get much better than this!"

Reprinted by permission of
Stephanie Piro ©2011.

92

Hearing the Voice of an Angel

By Hank Mattimore

Therefore, whoever takes the lowly position of this child
is the greatest in the kingdom of heaven.
~Matthew 18:4

There's a knock on my door. Phooey! "Grandpa Hank, I want to show you something." It's the wispy little voice of Serena, one of the foster kids.

"Honey, Grandpa is tired, and it's late."

It is nine o'clock and the end of a long summer day at the Children's Village. This old guy is pooped. Being a live-in surrogate grandpa to twenty-four foster kids is taking its toll. I've had kids around me all day. Timmy needed a one-on-one to finish writing a story. Marie and Sam wanted me to take them to the Dollar Store. Allison and Mimi brought over a vampire movie for me to watch. Tony and I went out for pizza. Mama mia! I love these little kids, but I don't want to see any of them for the rest of the day. It's time to close my door, have some lemonade, and watch the last two innings of the Giants game on TV.

"But I just want to show you something," she pleads.

Wearily, I give in. "Okay, but just for a minute."

Serena is a skinny little ten-year-old who could pass for about seven. She carries a song sheet in her hands. "Grandpa Hank, can I sing this song for you?" Her request startles me; I have never even heard her sing before, and kids her age are usually way too shy to sing in front of an adult. Intrigued, I sit down on my easy chair and wait for her to begin.

She blushes. "You can't look at me cuz I get embarrassed." Obediently, I look away. The little girl starts singing softly, almost in a whisper at first.

The more we get together, together, together,
The more we get together, the happier we'll be
For your friends are my friends, and my friends are your friends
The more we get together, the happier we'll be.

I listen to her small, thin voice, and little by little I feel the fatigue of the day melting away. It's the voice of an angel. I am honored that she chose to share this moment with me.

"Sweetheart, that was beautiful. Thank you for letting me hear you sing. You can sing to me anytime."

Serena beams shyly. Her little-girl face breaks into one of those winning, steal-your-soul kind of smiles. I want to give her a hug, but she is already headed for the door. "Thanks for listening to me," she calls out over her shoulder. "No, I should be thanking you…" I start to say, but she has already disappeared into her house next door.

Most of us experience some great moments in our lives—graduation days, first love, our wedding day, the birth of a child. These big moments give drama to our lives, but then there are the countless little moments. These are also part of who we are. For me, being an audience of one and listening to Serena's song was one of those God-given moments.

My Prayer

Thank you, God, for the gift of children. May their innocence touch our hearts and change us in sweet and simple ways. Their songs have the unique power to heal and bring us peace.

Amen.

93

In Everything Give Thanks

By Cynthia A. Lovely

Thanks be to God for his indescribable gift!
~2 Corinthians 9:15

I woke early Thanksgiving morning and turned to greet my husband, only to encounter an empty pillow. Strange. I knew he had come in late from his evening shift. I couldn't imagine why he would be up early. With a shrug, I dismissed the thought and focused on getting up to face the busy day.

Yawning, I flicked back the covers and stumbled to my feet. Mornings were difficult as my mother's illness progressed. Hospice care proved to be a tremendous help, with an aide visiting on weekdays. But my husband and I handled the rest of Mom's care. My mother, a precious, godly woman, loved the Lord and had brought us to the truth of the gospel. At this time of her life, I yearned to ease her discomfort, but exhaustion threatened to overtake me from the increasing responsibilities.

Memories from the previous night haunted me. Not one of my mother's better days, it had been a struggle to prepare her for bed. She tried to hide the grimace of pain that stole across her features. I went to bed and cried myself to sleep. Overwhelmed, overtired, and over the edge, I fell asleep, praying for strength to care for her and for grace to let her go.

With these thoughts rolling through my mind, I went to check on the current situation. Hopefully, her night had passed without incident. Half asleep, I fumbled my way downstairs. I heard voices in the kitchen, and when I walked in, I found my missing spouse.

Clad in his red worn-out terrycloth robe, his feet encased in hunting boots, and a faint growth of beard shadowing his face, he stood by the kitchen counter. He flashed me a grin while offering Mom a cup of coffee. I blinked the sleep from my eyes.

"What are you doing?" I asked.

Mom gazed at my husband with maternal-in-law pride as he gently steered me back toward the stairs.

"Let me be with your mom this morning. Go rest a bit longer," he said. A soft smile filtered through my weariness. I viewed his unique attire with a raised eyebrow. He grinned. "I had to let the dog out quick, and it was snowing." With a giggle, I kissed his scruffy cheek and headed back to the welcome comfort of my bed.

The kindness of my husband helped me realize how much I had to be thankful for, even in the midst of my troubles. My mother went home to be with the Lord a week after Thanksgiving. We had our final holiday meal together, and my only sister came home from out of town to surprise her. We were all with my mother when she gave her last breath.

Years later, I still remember finding my husband tending to Mom's needs even though he was as tired as I was at the time. I'm thankful for my husband, for God's faithfulness, and for His enduring strength. Truly, in everything we give God thanks.

My Prayer

*Father God, although I don't always recognize
your gifts, remind me of your goodness each
and every day. Open my eyes to all I have to
be thankful for, no matter what situation I find
myself in. And let my lips call forth a continual
thanksgiving, fulfilling the will of God.*

Amen.

94

Chocolate Comfort

By Sally Walls

When Jesus spoke again to the people, he said,
"I am the light of the world. Whoever follows me will never walk in darkness,
but will have the light of life."
~John 8:12

On a warm June evening, our lives were devastated by tragedy. Our eighteen-year-old son was killed cycling home from work in a bicycle-traffic accident. It happened several days after his high-school graduation, when plans and dreams for his life had seemed limitless. We asked ourselves, "Will we survive without him?"

An African proverb says, "It takes a village to raise a child." It also takes a village to bury a child. God, in His abundant faithfulness and mercy, surrounded us with caring community. We came to understand that He uses people to be His hands and feet.

Returning home from a road trip, I was overcome with sorrow. Our once-happy home had become a place of grieving; the walls cried out for Davis. His warm hugs and bright smile wouldn't be there to greet me, and I dreaded stepping inside.

Upon arrival, we noticed a brightly decorated box on our doorstep. We discovered freshly baked chocolate-chip cookies inside, still warm. Tucked alongside the cookies was a heartfelt note of encouragement from friends. With a cookie in each hand, I sat on my kitchen floor and wept. I was overcome with a sense of gratitude. God had provided a very tangible gift of love through their thoughtful gesture. We found such comfort in those cookies.

Nothing can diminish the enormity of our loss. It cuts like a knife. But we soon realized after Davis's passing that it was the small acts of kindness from others that helped us reclaim joy in our brokenness. Blessings come through giving. When we stop giving, we stop loving.

I now bake cookies to comfort those with heavy hearts. I appreciate that God wants to use my hands to share the joy of His love with others—even love in a chocolate-chip cookie.

My Prayer

Heavenly Father, thank you for your provision of comfort, hour by hour, day by day. Through your love, we are healing. We are learning to move through our brokenness by giving to others who are also hurting. You are a God of comfort and joy, and we trust you with our pain.

Amen.

95

Chicken Soup for the *Soul*

The Quilt

By Rosalie Grangaard Grosch

"Do not store up for yourselves treasures on earth,
where moth and rust destroy, and where thieves break in and steal.
But store up for yourselves treasures in heaven,
where moth and rust do not destroy, and where thieves do not break in and steal.
For where your treasure is, there your heart will be also."
~Matthew 6:19-21

Tears streamed down my face as I reminded myself, "It's only a thing."

Earlier in the day, the ringing of the telephone had startled us. It was the snowplow operator at our lake home. "I noticed that one window is broken and another is open."

With great haste, my husband set out on the hour-and-a-half drive. Not wanting to face the fear of the unknown, I stayed home.

Ken's call came. "They must have had lots of time because the place has been ransacked. They broke the bedroom window when they entered and exited with the loot through an open kitchen window."

Sawdust on the counter looked familiar to Ken. Checking the basement, he realized his chain saw was missing. That, along with other objects, must have been packed on the kitchen counter.

The drawers in the upstairs dressers were upside-down on the floor. Things were strewn around all over. A container of pennies was missing, as was the microwave from under the counter and guns from the closet.

With Ken's second phone call, I asked, "Is the quilt still there?"

"Just a minute. I will look." The phone was silent while I waited.

"It is gone. They must have wrapped everything in it when they fled."

I was heartbroken. That quilt meant everything to me. We were living out of the country when Mother died, and I was not able to attend her funeral. The quilt had been her project. Each piece told a story from my family's past. The partially finished quilt was given to my daughter. While at college, she finished the piecing. On an unforgettable trip to the other grandma's house, my two daughters and Grandma sat around the big frame, stitching everything by hand.

"We are doing this for Mom and Dad's twenty-fifth anniversary," our daughters sang as they stitched. In the center, embroidered in bright colors, was a special square: "Ken and Rosalie, 25 years of love and laughter."

We wept with joy when the quilt was presented to us. We pictured so many hands lovingly working: Mother cutting and piecing the old remnants; our daughter sewing the pieces between college classes; our two girls sitting around the quilt frame, stitching with Grandma.

Now, it was gone. I took off a day from work and went on a scavenger hunt, stopping at antique stores on the way to our cabin. No one had seen or heard anything of the quilt. I put up flyers with pictures asking people to call if they ran across the quilt.

I dream of someday finding a stained and worn quilt with our names stitched in the center. With a few left-over pieces, my daughter and I replicated the quilt in a smaller size. And as I look at those familiar fabric pieces, I give thanks.

My Prayer

Lord, it is hard to let go of things that mean so much. Help us to remember to cling close to that which truly matters—the love of others and the love that you have for us.

Amen.

96

Cakes for My King

By Sally Dixon

Therefore I glory in Christ Jesus in my service to God.
~Romans 15:17

I sat on the hard pew trying to concentrate on the minister's dron-
ing voice. My throat hurt, my body ached, and I was sure if I'd
peered in the mirror that I'd see a washed-out complexion. My
thoughts proved correct as a concerned friend whispered in my ear,
"Are you okay? You're as white as the flour you cook with." I merely
shrugged, allowing her words to stroke the self-pity wallowing inside
my soul. I closed my eyes, wishing I'd stayed home in bed.

For several weeks, I'd been working as a pastry chef in a new
business. The owner's grand plan included a cafe, restaurant, func-
tion centre, and hotel all rolled into one. And baking sweet creations
for them appeared to be a grand adventure. I bounced with excite-
ment the day I heard they wanted me to come. But five minutes after
walking through the door, disappointment arrived with a silent thud.
I walked into chaos—an undertrained, skeleton staff and a filthy,
grease-encrusted kitchen greeted me.

"It will improve with time," I told myself. I rolled up my sleeves
and started scrubbing the kitchen. "After all, it is a new business. Of
course, it will be hard work initially."

I went the extra mile by working ten-hour days, six days a week, but bedlam reigned, and my passion for cakes became a burden resulting in burnout.

But God had led me there. I'd felt sure of it... until now. Did I make a mistake? I wanted to throw down my wooden spoon and quit.

With a sigh, I slouched into the angular pew. I would quit. I couldn't be expected to work under these conditions.

"... Brother Lawrence worked in a monastery kitchen in the seventeenth century."

My eyes sprung open as the minister's voice penetrated my brain.

"His work was tedious — peeling potatoes and washing dishes."

I stared at the balding reverend.

"Revelation came to Brother Lawrence that everything he did should be done for the glory of God. Going about mundane tasks, he'd murmur, 'I put my little egg-cake into the frying pan for the love of God'" (from *The Practice of the Presence of God*).

The words speared my heart.

In that moment, I decided to persevere. The next day, as I whisked, stirred and baked, I continually muttered, "I put my little egg-cake into the frying pan..."

Crazy days tainted with exhaustion continued, but my attitude slowly changed. When self-pity came knocking, I'd picture that egg-cake sizzling in the pan. Then I told God my work was for Him. Eventually, as the business settled into normalcy, I made a discovery: I no longer concocted cakes with owners, customers or profit in mind. I baked cakes as if baking them for my King.

My Prayer

Heavenly Father, show me the path to walk.
When circumstances get tough, help me to
persevere and find strength in you. May the gifts
of my hands always bring you glory.

Amen.

97

Romance Shmo-mance

By Teresa Ambord

Nehemiah said, "Go and enjoy choice food and sweet drinks, and send some to those who have nothing prepared. This day is holy to our Lord. Do not grieve, for the joy of the LORD is your strength."
~Nehemiah 8:10

Here it is again—Valentine's Day. For couples, it can be a wonderful day, but for singles, not so much. It can be downright dismal.

As a divorced mother, I learned years ago to make plans for myself on special days like Christmas and my birthday. It kept me from falling into the holiday blues like so many singles do. But while my son was growing up, Valentine's Day didn't bother me much. Back then, it was mostly about buying something fun for him, helping him address valentines for his classmates, and making cupcakes to take to his school party.

Now, my son is twenty-seven and no longer at home. I've been single for twenty-five years, and the February focus on love and romance is really starting to bug me. A lot. I sneer at the commercials depicting a handsome husband surprising his wife with diamonds. I cringe at the silly sitcoms suggesting that anyone without a date on Valentine's Day must be a hairy ape. And as for those endless store displays of mushy cards, heart-shaped boxes of chocolates, and bouquets of roses... more than once I've contemplated mowing them down with my grocery cart. Accidentally, of course.

Yesterday, as I stood in line behind a young man who was buying one of those Valentine's bouquets, I thought to myself, "I can't wait till February fifteenth." Then a guy behind me leaned forward and asked the young man how much the roses cost. He wanted to buy some for his own wife. I smiled and said, "Smart husbands do things like that. You must be a smart husband." He sheepishly told me that it had taken him a while to learn to be "a smart husband."

As I thought about that, it brightened my spirits to think of this guy making his wife happy by presenting her with Valentine's flowers. That gave me an idea. Rather than getting depressed because I would not be getting roses or chocolate or diamonds or even a kiss, I decided to take the focus off myself by thinking of someone else with the same need. Immediately, I thought of three women in my church. They are lovely, godly women, but none of them has ever married. Like me, they would not be getting Valentine's gifts.

I went back into the store and bought four small, heart-shaped boxes of chocolates. Then I arranged to deliver them to my friends secretly. The fourth box, of course, was for me. No, it isn't the same as getting chocolate from a loving husband. But maybe, just for a moment, I brightened their spirits on Valentine's Day. It sure lifted mine.

My Prayer

*Heavenly Father, help me to remember that
my strength comes from your joy, not my
circumstances. Please make me aware
of the needs of those around me and
show me a way to help.*

Amen.

98

Our True Source

By Andrea Peebles

Therefore I tell you, whatever you ask for in prayer,
believe that you have received it, and it will be yours.
~Mark 11:24

I was fifty-two years old when I lost my job, and as much as we would like to believe that there are no prejudices where age is concerned, we all know that is simply not true.

I was devastated, to say the least. And even though I would get severance pay and unemployment for a while, the chances of me getting another job in the very competitive field of insurance were slim to none. I worried about the fact that I still had a mortgage on my home, a car payment, and several other incidental bills. How would we make it? My husband still had his job, but for the past twenty-four years it had taken both incomes, and it seemed we still barely got by.

During one of my many sleepless nights, I suddenly realized I was seeing only the human side of my dilemma. I was not looking to God as my true Source. I determined right then that I was going to put my trust and faith in Him.

I started by looking back over the tough times in my life when He had seen me through. I took account of the many times when what had looked impossible to me had somehow been taken care of by my one true Source. Then I remembered all the blessings in my life that I still had—my family, my health, my home—and began to feel grateful for all of them.

And, finally, as I thought about the One who held the moon in place and set the boundaries for the oceans, I began to pray—not for a job, as you might think, but only that He meet my needs as He had always done.

And, of course, He did.

I was unemployed for three years. But in those three years, I was able to focus on a part-time business of my own that was much more rewarding than any job I'd ever had in the corporate world. I totally replaced my previous "annual" salary with a part-time seasonal job with no commute. Unbelievably, while unemployed, we paid off the mortgage on our home and all of our incidental bills, and were able to buy the new car I needed for my business.

And, at fifty-five years old, I was hired for the best job I ever had in the same competitive field. And I went into it almost completely debt-free!

My Prayer

Dear Lord, help me to remember always that you are my source and my strength. If I place my trust in you, all things are possible.

Amen.

99

Chicken Soup for the Soul

Please Pass the Spaghetti

By Mary Z. Smith

So I commend the enjoyment of life, because there is nothing better for a person under the sun than to eat and drink and be glad.
~Ecclesiastes 8:15

"What are you having for dinner tonight?" I asked our daughter, Amber, over the phone. My question was answered with a drawn-out sigh.

"Oh, I think it's a spaghetti night." We both laughed at her response.

When our two daughters were in their teens, we'd faced some challenging times with health issues, career changes, and my husband traveling quite a bit.

One evening as I chatted with my own mother long-distance, I'd suddenly grown serious.

"Mom, what's the secret to putting a little joy into family life? You know how hard it is juggling careers and raising teenagers. Sometimes, it gets a little intense around here."

Mom's words were as surprising as a visit from an unexpected guest.

"Whisper a prayer... then toss some spaghetti at each other once in a while… cooked, that is… Keep things light. Make each other laugh."

That evening, I served pasta for dinner, sharing Mom's advice with my husband and the girls. Mom's idea sounded crazy, even to my own ears. We filled our plates with food, and started sharing our concerns over homework assignments and scheduled appointments for the week ahead. My phone conversation with Mom seemed all but forgotten.

Or so I thought…

As the conversation grew more and more intense, I spotted Amber bowing her head, then reaching for the bowl of spaghetti resting in the center of the table.

"That's odd. Her plate is already full," I pondered silently.

Suddenly, she sunk her fingers into the soft pasta. Lifting several long strands from the bowl, she tossed them high into the air before releasing a loud "Wheeeeee!"

Her actions were met with stunned silence. As we gazed up at the strands of spaghetti dangling from the ceiling, sudden laughter emerged like a volcanic eruption. Throughout the rest of the meal and well into the night, our family experienced one of the happiest, laidback times we'd had in years.

Our daughters, Autumn and Amber, are both married now with families of their own. Thankfully, we're blessed with more days filled with happiness than sadness. But on those days when life becomes a little too intense, we know what to do…

Whisper a little prayer and pass the spaghetti.

My Prayer

*Father God, when our lives are out of balance,
we look to you to put everything back into
perspective. Your awesome power calms our
emotions and restores our sense of well-being.
How wonderful it is that even in the midst of
chaos, you are a God who appreciates
a good laugh.*

Amen.

"I hope God likes spaghetti ... because Grandma said to pray before tossing it!"

Reprinted by permission of Stephanie Piro ©2011.

A Merry Heart

By Jennifer Smith

A cheerful heart is good medicine, but a crushed spirit dries up the bones.
~Proverbs 17:22

Mother's Day was quickly approaching. Like many people, we had been adversely affected by the economy. Living paycheck to paycheck, our savings account evaporated into thin air. There was no extra money for anything. It has always been a tradition for Easter that I get a new dress to parade around in like a vain peacock. Well, when I became a mother for the first time, my husband thought it only appropriate to get me a new dress on Mother's Day, as well. But I knew that no new dress would be coming for me this year. We had been creative in making eggs into fifteen different recipes, and hot dogs were our new T-bone steak. Life had thrown us some lemons and, frankly, we weren't lemonade drinkers.

I tried not to get discouraged. "Our rainbow will come soon," I kept assuring myself, but it seemed that lightning struck everywhere I stood. I was getting tired of being frazzled and squeezing every bit out of those lemons.

Mother's Day was my day — a whole day dedicated to me — and I was dreading it. When I woke up that day, the only thought I could muster was, "What kind of eggs will I make today?" But there was a card on the table. On the outside of the envelope it stated, "Enclosed is a few dollars for a new dress. Enjoy." My heart started pitter-pattering twice as quickly as normal, and I thought, "Craig must have been setting money aside."

I opened the card and pulled out a check for one thousand dollars! In the memo, it stated that the money was for a new dress and shoes. I've never spent more than fifty dollars on a dress, so I knew something was up. I looked on the back of the envelope, and it stated, "P.S. Please don't cash for three more years."

I burst into laughter. But as I read the card, my husband's words were so warm and encouraging that I began to cry. We went to church that day, and although I was in old clothes, I radiated with joy and gratitude because I was clothed in love and laughter. I found that I was rich, even living on eggs. After that day, I began squeezing those lemons cheerfully, and soon we all enjoyed the taste of lemonade. I found this plaque at a store and put it in our home: "The happiest people don't necessarily have the best of everything; they just make the best of everything they have."

My Prayer

Father, thank you for the medicinal power in laughter. Thank you that, even in difficult times, we can be optimistic, have joy, and laugh. May we find ourselves making the best out of whatever situation you place us in.

Amen.

Just Laugh

By Tracy Crump

He will yet fill your mouth with laughter and your lips with shouts of joy.
~Job 8:21

"I like being around people who know how to laugh," my mother-in-law exclaimed on a family outing for her eighty-fifth birthday. "If you can't laugh, you might as well be dead." Fairsee's laughter filled the air that afternoon as she walked the grounds of a Civil War park, keeping up with her twenty-something grandson.

Many people would say Fairsee had little to laugh about. My husband, Stan, was just an infant when Fairsee's life spiraled out of control. First, her adoring father died suddenly. On the day of her father's funeral, Fairsee's husband became so ill with tonsillitis that he could not attend the service and required surgery shortly thereafter. He never awoke from anesthesia, succumbing to an undiagnosed brain tumor. Reeling from shock, the young widow clung to the promise of new life that grew within her—she was pregnant with their second child. But a few weeks later, joy again turned to sorrow when she went into premature labor. The baby died twenty-four hours after birth. Within a three-month span, Fairsee buried a parent, a spouse, and a child—the three most devastating losses anyone could experience.

Fairsee did not have the luxury of lingering in grief, however. She still had a baby to care for. At a time when most women stayed home with their children, she was forced to return to work as a hairdresser to provide for them both. Money was tight, so she gave up her car and walked to work. Never to own a home as she had always dreamed, she and Stan moved into less and less expensive rental housing and did without many things others considered necessities.

Faced with so many losses, Fairsee could have chosen to be sad and bitter, but she focused instead on God's blessings. "I have a healthy baby. My job supplies enough food and a place to live. God doesn't want me to be a 'gloomy Gus.' He gave me the gift of laughter, and I'm going to use it." She commenced every day with prayer, faced each trial as it came, and left the rest up to God. Instead of crying, she chose to laugh.

Through the years, Fairsee has continued to delight her family with laughter. My sons still remember the time their Gran stepped out onto the front porch to tell us goodbye and began laughing so hard over a joke that she lost her balance. We watched, frozen in horror, as she somersaulted over a three-foot hedge and landed unhurt on the ground below—still laughing.

Tragedies come to us all. Often, our attitudes make the difference in whether we flounder in despair or reach for the joy of the Lord. Sometimes, the best thing to do is what Fairsee did—just laugh.

My Prayer

Lord, please keep my eyes focused on your blessings and help me remember the gift of laughter, even in the midst of life's trials. Let my laughter lift someone else's heart and reflect the joy that only you can bestow.

Amen.

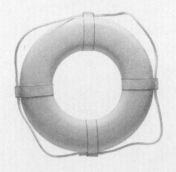

Devotional Stories for Tough Times

Meet Our Contributors

Teresa Ambord was an accountant for many years before becoming a full-time writer. Now she writes full-time from her home in far northern California, surrounded by her posse of small dogs, including foster pets. Teresa makes a living writing for business, but her heart is in writing about family.

Monica A. Andermann lives on Long Island with her husband Bill and their cat Charley. She is a frequent contributor to the *Chicken Soup for the Soul* series and more of her writing can be found both online and in a variety of print media.

Karen Asire has a Bachelor's degree in Piano Pedagogy and a Master's degree in Counseling. In addition to teaching piano, Karen has published several inspirational articles as well as a book, *Acquainted with Grief*. Karen also has a story in *Chicken Soup for the Soul: Devotional Stories for Mothers*. She resides in South Carolina.

Rita Billbe owns Angels Retreat on the White River in Arkansas. Her passions are fly fishing and singing in her church choir. She has stories in five other *Chicken Soup for the Soul* books, a suspense novel completed and a blog: www.flyfishing4faith.com.

Jennie Bradstreet is a freelance writer. She is a wife and mother and has been a stay-at-home mom for sixteen years. Her family has gone through many struggles and adventures including a premature baby, a house fire, three floods and cancer, all of which have given Jennie a unique perspective on life. E-mail her at bejennie@msn.com.

Robin A. Bridges received her Bachelor of Science degree from Buffalo State College in 1995. She loves hanging out with her family and passionately enjoys photography and writing. E-mail her at rsbridges@roadrunner.com.

Dianne E. Butts has over 250 publications in magazines and books, is the author of *Deliver Me: Hope, Help, & Healing through True Stories of Unplanned Pregnancy* (www.DeliverMeBook.com), and is an aspiring screenwriter. She enjoys riding her motorcycle with her husband Hal and gardening with her cat in Colorado. www.DianneEButts.com.

Sally Clark lives and writes in Fredericksburg, TX. Her award-winning poetry and stories have been featured in anthologies and gift books published by Tyndale House Publishers, Thomas Nelson, Howard Books, New World Library, FaithWords, Adams Media, and Chronicle Books. This is her third contribution to the *Chicken Soup for the Soul* series. Learn more at www.sallyclark.info.

Phyllis Cochran lives in Winchendon, MA, with her husband Philip. She continues to write inspirational stories whenever she experiences them. She has two grown children, five grandchildren and two great grandchildren. E-mail her at pacwriter@verizon.net.

Liz Cook is a registered nurse, wife, mother and grandmother of six grandsons. Her writing began as a hobby, which has progressed to writing for a local newspaper and several nursing journals. She enjoys time with her family and The United Methodist Church that her husband pastors.

Leslie Cooper has a non-profit organization which includes teaching caregivers, teachers, doctors, therapists, etc. how to make and apply adaptive devices to enable disabled users to gain independence. It is about one-fourth of the cost to make them versus buying them. Her son demonstrates at the presentations and workshops.

An avid writer since childhood, **Florence Crago** writes primarily about her family life experiences. She and husband Glen served as pastors, college professors, social workers, and volunteers for Heifer International, until his death in 2000. Currently she is a chaplain at the retirement community where she lives and leads a writers group.

Tracy Crump has numerous published credits. She is a CLASS graduate, moderates an online critique group, and enjoys teaching other writers at conferences and through her Write Life Workshops. She was recently promoted to "Grandma" and will talk about Nellie to anyone who listens. Visit Tracy at www.TracyCrump.com.

Barbara Cueto is an evangelist first. Her autobiography, *From Mafia Princess to God's Princess*, is sold in Spanish in over thirty countries. She writes, speaks and sings for her savior Jesus Christ, in whose service she is employed full-time. Contact her at www.BarbaraCuetoMinistries.com.

Michele Cushatt writes stories from a vast collection of life experiences, many of which helped forge her deep love of words. Now she writes and speaks full-time, encouraging others to celebrate life even when it's difficult. Michele, her husband, and three teenage boys live in Colorado. E-mail Michele at michele@michelecushatt.com.

Christina D'Agostino received her Bachelor of Science with honors from Mount St. Mary's University in 2009. She teaches second and sixth graders in a Catholic school. She loves running, service work, and her family and friends.

Regina K. Deppert graduated from Florida Metropolitan University. She now works in the legal field and lives in Indiana, where she grew up. Regina enjoys reading, writing, music and animals. She hopes to write more. E-mail her at gina92262@msn.com.

Denise A. Dewald has been writing Christian material for over twenty-five years with numerous publications to her name. Denise enjoys reading, needlework, music, her family and pets. One of her poems has been made into a song and aired on Family Life Radio. E-mail her at denise_a_dewald@yahoo.com.

Sally Dixon received a Bachelor of Education in 1999 and a Post Graduate Diploma in Creative Writing from Tabor Adelaide in 2011. She is a freelance writer from Australia. She loves traveling and once worked as a pastry chef in England. She desires to write children's books and biographies.

Although **Janet Perez Eckles** lost her sight, she gained insight to serve as an international speaker, writer, columnist and author of *Simply Salsa: Dancing without Fear at God's Fiesta*, Judson Press, August 2011. From her home in Florida she imparts inspiration at www.inspirationforyou.com.

Judi Folmsbee is a retired teacher after twenty-five years of teaching elementary special education. She has written three children's books and many devotionals. She has been published in church booklets and religious and secular newspapers. She enjoys photography, gardening, scrapbooking, and family time.

Peggy Purser Freeman is the author of *The Coldest Day in Texas*, *Swept Back to a Texas Future* and stories in *Chicken Soup for the Soul: Teens Talk Middle School* and *Chicken Soup for the Soul: Happily Ever After*. She is currently editor for *Granbury Showcase Magazine*. Learn more at www.peggypurserfreeman.com.

Carol Gibson, graduate of the Christian Writer's Guild Apprentice Level Program, is a registered nurse at a correctional facility. She has written stories for reading textbooks and authored eight children's stories not yet published. She loves to make heirloom quilts and write for God. E-mail her at c.gibson1017@yahoo.com.

Pamela Gilsenan is the proud mother of five adult children and assorted grandchildren. For decades, food service industry jobs supported her while she wrote articles and books. E-mail her at P_Gilsenan@hotmail.com.

Arlene Rains Graber's first devotional book, *Devoted to Traveling*, was released in 2010. She has won numerous awards for memoirs and non-fiction articles including Writer of the Year, and Article of the Year from East Wichita News, and First Place in the Heart of American Christian Writers contest. Learn more at arlenerainsgraber.com.

Lynne Graham-Orlando has written two children's books and is currently working on three Christian-fiction novels in hopes of publishing them soon. Born in England, she resides in Michigan, is happily married, and is a mom of three and grandmom of two. She enjoys writing, cooking, gardening and kayaking. E-mail her at mrslynn@ymail.com.

Rosalie Grangaard Grosch received a B.A. from Luther College, Decorah, IA. She has taught in the United States, Ethiopia, Papua New Guinea and China. Rosalie is an inspirational speaker and small group leader. She enjoys travel, fellowship in her faith community, a lake home, friends and family.

Linda A. Haywood received both her Bachelor of Social Work and Master of Social Work degrees from Eastern Michigan University. She has worked with seniors, those receiving mental health services and survivors of domestic violence. Linda plans to write inspirational books for adults. E-mail her at lhaywood45@yahoo.com.

David Heeren has authored or co-authored twelve books. His latest book, *In His Steps Again*, is an update of the 1896 Charles Sheldon classic. He also has written *The Sign of His Coming*, concerning the celestial sign of the Second Coming of Jesus Christ. E-mail him at enoch7@comcast.net.

Rhonda Hensley resides in Spartanburg, SC, with her husband Gary, a Southern Baptist pastor. She is an Inspirational Speaker and Bible Teacher for Women's Ministries. She also enjoys freelance writing and photography. Learn more at www.kingdomjewelsministry.com.

Darlene Hierholzer is the mother of three children, unexpectedly losing her beloved son, David, in 2008. She worked with her daughter, Dana Hierholzer, the author of this piece, to share a story of a comforting soul during that heartbreaking time. Currently, she is helping her daughter with her first novel, *Something to Believe In*.

Ann Holbrook lives in Northwest Arkansas. She has been published in *The Storyteller*; *The Ozarks Mountaineer*; anthologies including: *Writing on Walls*, *Voices*, *Echoes of the Ozarks*, *Skipping Stones*, and *Chicken Soup for the Soul: Tough Times, Tough People*. She is working on an inspirational book for cancer patients and their families.

Helen Hoover enjoys sewing, knitting, and traveling. She and her husband volunteer with the Sower Ministry for retired Christian RV'ers. Word Aflame Publishing, The Secret Place, WordAction Publishing, The Quiet Hour, Light and Life Communications, Victory in Grace, and *The Lutheran Digest* have published her devotionals and personal articles.

Ken Hornok, ThM (Dallas Theological Seminary) pastors Midvalley Bible Church in Salt Lake City and is an adjunct professor with several publishing credits. He and Marcia raised six children, who now reward them with grandchildren. Having run thirteen marathons, he also bikes, hunts, gardens, raises bees, and fixes things.

Teresa Hoy enjoys life in rural Missouri with her husband and a large family of rescued cats and dogs. She writes freelance articles, fiction, and poetry. Several of her stories have appeared in the *Chicken Soup for the Soul* series, *The Ultimate* series, and other anthologies. Visit her at www.teresahoy.com.

Mary Hughes loves writing true stories that encourage and inspire people to live more faith-filled lives. She has a devotional newsletter, "Christian Potpourri," now in its eighth year. E-mail her at christianpotpourri@hotmail.com or visit her website at christianpotpourri.com.

This is a true story taken from **Corinne A. Hummel's** daily life. Her sister, Marie Senter of San Antonio, helped her write it.

Aura Imbarus, PhD, is the author of the Pulitzer Prize entry *Out of the Transylvania Night*. Born and raised in Sibiu/Hermannstadt, Romania, or more precisely in "Dracula's county—Transylvania," she works as a motivational speaker and expert in educational strategies and methodologies. Learn more at www.auraimbarus.com or contact her via e-mail at auraimbarus@yahoo.com.

Robbie Iobst is a writer and speaker living in Centennial, CO, with her husband John, son Noah and puggle Scooby. Her stories have appeared in several *Chicken Soup for the Soul* books. E-mail Robbie at robbieiobst@hotmail.com or learn more at www.robbieiobst.com.

Terry Ann Johnson has embraced writing since her youth in West Plains, MO. She is a proud wife, mother, and grandmother. While working as a copywriter, Terry is continuing her writing career as both an aspiring screenwriter and novelist. Terry enjoys spending time with her family, reading, and the outdoors.

Nancy B. Kennedy is a long-time writer and editor. Her latest book is *Miracles and Moments of Grace: Inspiring Stories from Military Chaplains* (Leafwood Publishers, 2011). She has also published two books containing children's science activities. To learn more visit her website at www.nancybkennedy.com.

Carolyn K. Knefely is a speaker, etiquette specialist and career coach. As a people polisher and co-director of Christian Communicators, she educates, validates and launches women in their speaking ministries through conferences, retreats and workshops. She delivers entertaining and interactive mother/daughters teas and retreats. Learn more at www.teacupliving.blogspot.com.

Kathleen Kohler is a writer and speaker from the Pacific Northwest. Her articles, rooted in personal experience, appear in books and internationally in magazines. She and her husband have three children and seven grandchildren. She enjoys bird watching, gardening, traveling, and painting. Learn more at www.kathleenkohler.com.

Laurie Kolp has a Bachelor of Science in Curriculum and Instruction from Texas A&M University. She taught school for twelve years and although she continues tutoring children with dyslexia, her true love is writing. Laurie lives in Southeast Texas with her husband, three children and two dogs. Contact her at www.conversationswithacardinal. blogspot.com.

Madeleine Kuderick is passionate about writing stories and poems that touch the heart. Her work appears in *Chicken Soup for the Soul*, *A Cup of Comfort*, Hallmark Gift Books and similar anthologies. She speaks at conferences hosted by the International Reading Association and the Council for Learning Disabilities. Learn more at www.madeleinekuderick.com.

Dorothy LaMantia writes stories of everyday faith and redemption in her study overlooking Barnegat Bay, NJ. A former English teacher, she has won an award for reporting from the Catholic Press Association. This is her third contribution to the *Chicken Soup for the Soul* series. E-mail her at dotelama@aol.com.

Kathryn Lay is an author of many children's books as well as stories and articles for children and adults. She and her family live in Texas. Learn more at kathrynlay.com or e-mail her at rlay15@aol.com.

Jamie Lee operates Animal Bonds, a holistic wellness program for dogs. Jamie helps "add years to your dog's life, and life to your dog's years." Jamie has been published in *Chicken Soup for the Soul: My Dog's Life* and national pet magazines. Learn more about her at AnimalBondsLV.com.

Janeen Lewis is a freelance writer living in central Kentucky with her husband and two young children. She has a degree in Journalism from Eastern Kentucky University and has previously been published in seven *Chicken Soup for the Soul* anthologies. E-mail her at jlewis0402@netzero.net.

Cynthia A. Lovely, from New York, is a freelance writer and musician, also active in church ministry. Published in various magazines, newspapers and anthologies, she is a member of American Christian Fiction Writers and currently working on a contemporary woman's novel. E-mail her at cllyrics@gmail.com or visit www.cynthialovely.com.

Melanie Marks has had over fifty stories in magazines such as *Highlights*, *Woman's World* and *Teen Magazine*. She's had four children's books published, and numerous teen novels including: *The Dating Deal*, *A Demon's Kiss*, *Paranormal Punch*, and *The Stranger Inside*. Learn more at byMelanieMarks.com or e-mail her at melanie@byMelanieMarks.com.

Hank Mattimore is currently a volunteer surrogate grandpa for a Children's Village in California. A widower, Hank has two grandchildren of his own as well as the twenty-four foster children who live at the Village.

Before she even learned to write her name, **Ann McArthur** was dictating stories to her mother, who patiently typed them. She graduated from seminary and continues to tell stories in the women's Bible studies that she teaches. She is about to release her first novel, *Choking on a Camel*.

Jeri McBryde lives in a small town outside of Memphis, TN. She recently retired from the library system and spends her days reading and working on her dream of being a published writer. Jeri loves crocheting and chocolate. Her family and faith are the center of her life. This is her second story to appear in the *Chicken Soup for the Soul* series. E-mail her at jeri47@bellsouth.net.

Jennifer McDonald has been a military spouse for twenty-three years and has been stationed around the world, currently living in Hawaii. A homeschooling mother of four, she has written numerous articles for homeschooling and military spouse publications. You can find her blog at www.afjen.blogspot.com or e-mail her at stevejen88@googlemail.com.

Michelle Close Mills' stories have appeared in many anthologies including *Chicken Soup for the Soul in Menopause*, *Chicken Soup for the Soul: My Cat's Life*, and *Chicken Soup for the Soul: Devotional Stories for Mothers*. A former native of Fort Wayne, IN, Michelle and her family live in central Florida. Learn more at www.authorsden.com/michelleclosemills.

Katie A. Mitchell received her Bachelor of Arts in English, with honors, from Missouri State University in 1979. She is in corporate public relations for a major outdoors company and enjoys hiking, singing, antiquing and volunteering with children's organizations.

Kevin Morrison is a 1992 graduate of Warren High School in Downey, CA, and a veteran of the U.S. Air Force. Now a stay-at-home dad and aspiring Christian novelist in Bakersfield, CA, he and his wife are gladly busy with the activities of their four children. E-mail Kevin at 2kings617@gmail.com.

Adjunct reference librarian **Shelley Mosley** has co-written nine books and one novella. She also writes articles and reviews books for professional journals. One of her stories, "Man and Car: A Love Story," was in *Chicken Soup for the Soul: Family Matters*. E-mail her at deborahshelley@mindspring.com.

Herchel E. Newman, professional firefighter, began writing after retirement. He is often called upon for his storytelling talent. He enjoys photography as a business and hobby. He is also a motorcycling enthusiast. He and his wife are marriage mentors and love being grandparents. E-mail Herchel at ZoomN500@juno.com.

Tammy Nischan is a Christian teacher, speaker, and writer who resides in Grayson, KY, with her husband, Tim. She is the mother to four children on earth and two in heaven. Tammy enjoys sharing her photography and devotional thoughts on her blog, "My Heart… His Words." Learn more at www.tammynischan.blogspot.com.

Maria Norris graduated from The Ohio State University with a degree in Journalism. After moving to Southern California, she held various writing, editing and sales positions. She retired to North Texas in 2008 to be near family, and enjoys writing children's books and poems. E-mail her at marianorris@sbcglobal.net.

Carrie O'Maley received her Bachelor of Arts in Journalism from Butler University and Master of Library Science from Indiana University. She works as a public librarian. This story is dedicated to family and friends who remind her to live with faith, hope, and love. E-mail her at omaleyc@yahoo.com.

Christa Holder Ocker, a repeat contributor, likes to write about everyday life. Her memoir *auf Wiedersehen*, a 2010 Finalist in the

ForeWord Book of the Year Award, has been added to the Holocaust Collection at Yeshiva University, the Leo Baeck Institute, The New York Society Library, and the Goethe Institut.

Charles Owens hails from Trinity, NC. He received his undergraduate degree in business from Point Loma Nazarene College in San Diego and his Master's degree from the Naval War College. Charles and his wife Sonja have three children and enjoy traveling and working in Christian ministry.

David Ozab is currently writing his first non-fiction book, *Her Name is Anna*, which tells the story of his daughter's cleft surgery and struggles with speech. This devotional is excerpted from his book. He also writes about his life as a stay-at-home dad at FatherhoodEtc.com.

Sheri Palivoda received her Bachelor of Science and Master's degree in Education from Indiana University of Pennsylvania. She is currently working as a school librarian in Pittsburgh, PA. She believes that reading is the foundation for all academic subjects, and she is currently working on several children's books.

Andrea Peebles lives with her husband of thirty-four years. She has worked in the insurance industry for over twenty-seven years and currently operates a part-time garden wedding facility in Rockmart, GA. She enjoys travel, photography, cooking, reading and of course, writing. E-mail her at aanddpeebles@aol.com.

Stephanie Piro is a cartoonist, illustrator and designer. She is one of King Features' team of women cartoonists, "Six Chix" (she is the Saturday chick). She also does the cartoon panel "Fair Game." Her work appears all over, from books to greeting cards. In addition, she designs gift items for her company Strip T's and her CafePress Shop. Learn more at www.stephaniepiro.com.

Jennifer Quasha is a freelance writer and editor who has focused on pets since 1998. She has written for many *Chicken Soup for the Soul* books and recently co-authored *Chicken Soup for the Soul: My Dog's Life* and *Chicken Soup for the Soul: My Cat's Life*. She lives with her two dogs, Sugar and Scout. Learn more at www.jenniferquasha.com.

Brenda Redmond is blessed with two daughters and a wonderful husband who inspire her every day. She enjoys traveling, reading, swimming, camping and spending time with family and friends. She plans to continue to write and grow as a writer. E-mail her at brendaswriting@hotmail.ca.

Crystal Brennan Ruzicka grew up in Fairport, NY, and currently resides in Chippewa Falls, WI, with her husband and ten children. She enjoys spending time with her family and writing her devotional blog, "Not My Steps." She can be contacted through her blog at http://notmysteps.blogspot.com.

Theresa Sanders considers it an honor to be a frequent Chicken Soup for the Soul contributor. An award-winning technical writer and consultant, she lives with her husband in suburban St. Louis and is blessed with four beloved grown children. E-mail her at TheresaLSanders@charter.net.

Cyndi S. Schatzman, RN, MS, CCRN, a former nursing instructor and critical care nurse, is currently an inspirational speaker and author. She is married to her college sweetheart Todd and has three children who have grown into young adulthood despite the fact that their mother still burns garlic toast. Contact Cyndi for your next speaking engagement at mustangok@earthlink.net.

Lindy Schneider is a children's book illustrator, author and inspirational speaker. She speaks on how to discover God's presence in everyday experiences. This is her third story to be published in the *Chicken Soup for the Soul* series. E-mail her at lindy_schn@yahoo.com or learn more about Lindy at www.LindysBooks.com.

Dayle Shockley is an award-winning writer, the author of three books, and a contributor to many other works, including the *Chicken Soup for the Soul* series. She and her retired fire captain husband can often be found traveling around the country, enjoying God's handiwork. Visit Dayle's website for more information at www.dayleshockley.com.

Jennifer Smith is a nursing student who is passionate about life and writing. She loves to spend time with her wonderful husband and her two sons. She hopes that her stories will point the readers to Christ and that He alone will be glorified.

Mary Z. Smith is a regular contributor to *Chicken Soup for the Soul* books as well as *Guideposts* and *Angels on Earth* magazines. Her most recent book, *Life's A Symphony*, is dedicated to her niece's husband Lou who gave his life serving our country. Mary enjoys walking, gardening and spending time praising God.

Diane Stark is a former teacher turned stay-at-home mom and free-lance writer. She loves to write about the important things in life: her family and her faith. Diane is the author of *Teachers' Devotions to Go*. E-mail her at DianeStark19@yahoo.com.

Michelle Stewart pastors with her husband at a multi-national church in Canada. She is mom to five kids—plus one waiting in heaven! She leads "girlfriends," a ministry for women and is the founder/organizer of Pink Christmas. One of her favorite places is on a beach—reading. E-mail her at michstew@rogers.com.

Kim Stokely has toured throughout the country in a one-person musical about women in the Bible. In addition to stories in the *Chicken Soup for the Soul* books and *Vista*, her fiction works have been printed in *Writers' Journal*. She is currently working on her fourth novel. She blogs at www.kimstokely.com.

Sandra Diane Stout received her Associate's degree in Business

Studies from Indiana University Kokomo and is a graduate of the Institute of Children's Literature. She is a secretary at Indiana University Kokomo. Diane enjoys directing church drama, designing costumes, and is an accomplished pianist. She writes children's non-fiction. E-mail her at dstout@iuk.edu.

Cozy mystery author **Ann Summerville** was born in England, and in search of a warmer climate, moved to California before settling in Texas. Ann is a member of Trinity Writers' Workshop and resides in Fort Worth with her son, two boisterous dogs and a somewhat elusive cat. Learn more at www.AnnSummerville.com.

Sue Tornai completed "What's Your Story?" apprentice writing course with the Christian Writers Guild in 2004. Her articles and stories have been published in Christian magazines and anthologies. Sue teaches Sunday school and enjoys camping and fishing with her husband John and dog Maggie. E-mail her at suetornai@ymail.com.

Marilyn Turk received her B.A. in Journalism from LSU and has been published in *The Upper Room*, *Guideposts*, *Clubhouse Jr.*, and *Coastal Christian Family*. Besides writing, she enjoys the Florida panhandle lifestyle—walking, playing tennis, gardening and fishing with her husband Chuck. She is currently writing two inspirational novels. E-mail her at marilynturkwriter@yahoo.com.

Shirley Pieters Vogel is a respected inspirational speaker and author whose articles have appeared in many publications including *Leadership Journal*. Her prize-winning book, *wHispers*, was published in 2008. Shirley's passion is to share God's love, hope and faithfulness with those who are struggling. E-mail her at whispers@shirleyvogel.com or visit www.shirleyvogel.com.

Sally Walls has not been a spectator to loss; she has been fully engaged. Throughout a decade of heartache, God has shown her that He makes good on all of His promises. Sally, her husband James, and teenage son Owen live in Calgary, Canada. Their other son, Davis, now lives in heaven.

Whether through words or photographs, **Cari Weber** is passionate about telling stories. She is a freelance writer and award-winning photographer whose work has been published in several books and magazines. Cari finds beauty in the ordinary and enjoys nature and wildlife. Learn more at www.cariweber.com, or e-mail her at cari.weber@yahoo.com.

B. Lee White has been a licensed practical nurse for nineteen years and a writer since she could write her first words. She is currently going to college to become a registered nurse and is working on her third book in the *Soulfinder* series. She enjoys reading, writing, and singing.

After fifteen years in the nuclear medicine field, **Melissa Wootan** made the decision to change careers and became a full-time wife and mother. She is currently at work writing a children's humorous book series. E-mail her at 4wootans@gmail.com.

Sandy Wright works with gifted and talented students and is a freelance writer. She loves hiking, snowshoeing, horses, traveling, and rollicking with her yellow Lab, Jake. Though at times her life has been challenging, she embraces it with joy. E-mail her at wrightonsandy@yahoo.com.

Meet Our Authors

Susan M. Heim is a longstanding author and editor, specializing in parenting, women's and Christian issues. After the birth of her twin boys in 2003, Susan left her desk job as a Senior Editor at a publishing company and has never looked back. Being a work-at-home mother allows her to follow her two greatest passions: parenting and writing.

Susan's published books include *Chicken Soup for the Soul: New Moms*; *Chicken Soup for the Soul: Devotional Stories for Mothers*; *Chicken Soup for the Soul: Family Matters*; *Chicken Soup for the Soul: Devotional Stories for Women*; *Chicken Soup for the Soul: All in the Family*; *Chicken Soup for the Soul: Twins and More*; *Boosting Your Baby's Brain Power*; *It's Twins! Parent-to-Parent Advice from Infancy Through Adolescence*; *Oh, Baby! 7 Ways a Baby Will Change Your Life the First Year*; and, *Twice the Love: Stories of Inspiration for Families with Twins, Multiples and Singletons*. She is also working on a fiction book for teens and young adults.

Susan's articles and stories have appeared in many books, websites, and magazines, including *TWINS Magazine* and *Angels on Earth*. She writes a parenting blog, "Susan Heim on Parenting," at http://susanheim.blogspot.com. And she is the founder of TwinsTalk, a website with tips, advice and stories about raising twins and multiples, at www.twinstalk.com.

Susan and her husband Mike are the parents of four active sons, who are in elementary school and college! You can reach Susan at susan@susanheim.com and visit her website at www.susanheim.com. Join her on Twitter and Facebook by searching for ParentingAuthor.

Karen C. Talcott is the co-author of the devotional books published by Chicken Soup for the Soul, including *Chicken Soup for the Soul: Devotional Stories for Women* and *Chicken Soup for the Soul: Devotional Stories for Mothers*. Her work was also included in *Chicken Soup for the Soul: Twins and More*. She has a variety of new projects in the works, including several children's books and many more devotional short stories.

Karen's experience in writing came from fifteen years in the classroom and a master's degree in curriculum from Oregon State University. In addition to teaching classes in grades 3-6, Karen was instrumental in setting school curriculum at the school district in which she taught. While no longer teaching elementary school, Karen continues to share her experiences and knowledge through her writing and speaking engagements.

After the birth of her twins and caring for a two-and-a-half-year-old daughter, Karen decided to focus her attention on freelance writing. Her husband, Leland, and three children, Kara, Griffin, and Taylor, are very supportive of her writing, and for this she is thankful. She is also a member of the Society of Children's Book Writers and Illustrators.

Born in the beautiful state of Oregon, Karen now resides in Florida. She finds her best inspiration comes in the morning on her long walks with her two Golden Retrievers. Story ideas and titles seem to flow as she communes in God's world. In her spare time, what precious moments there are, she enjoys her children and their many sports and activities, gardening, walking, and faithfully attending her local church. She can be reached at Kartalcott@aol.com.

About Mary Beth Chapman

Mary Beth Chapman is the wife of Grammy and Dove Award winning recording artist, Steven Curtis Chapman. Steven and Mary Beth were married in 1984 and have six children, including three little girls adopted from China. They met in college after being assigned the same mailbox because they had the same last name. (Mary Beth's maiden name was Chapman.)

For years, the Chapman family had strongly supported friends and organizations that were involved in adoption, but they had no idea how much their role would grow. Mary Beth never dreamed she'd adopt a child, let alone one from so far away. In fact, she was the lone dissenter for most of the two-and-a-half-year campaign that daughter Emily staged to get her parents to adopt a baby from overseas. Once Mary Beth got on board with the adoption, she did so with zeal!

After adopting Shaohannah in 2000, the Chapmans followed suit in 2002 by adopting Stevey Joy, and Maria Sue in 2004. Tragically, in May 2008, Maria was accidentally killed when she was struck by an SUV in the Chapmans' driveway. The family has gone on to share their story of deep sorrow and renewed hope with the world through interviews with such outlets as *People*, *Good Morning America*, and *Larry King Live*.

Touched and forever transformed by the miracle of adoption,

Steven and Mary Beth began the non-profit ministry, Show Hope, a movement to care for orphans. Originally named Shaohannah's Hope after their first adopted daughter, Show Hope mobilizes individuals and communities to meet the most pressing needs of orphans by providing homes for waiting children through adoption aid grants, as well as life-saving medical care for orphans with special needs. Additionally, Show Hope empowers families, churches, and communities with adoption and orphan care resources and advocacy efforts.

To date, Show Hope is now an internationally recognized voice for orphan advocacy and has given more than 2,700 financial grants, affecting the lives of children from 46 different countries, including the U.S. Mary Beth currently serves as the president of Show Hope, and together she and Steven promote adoption awareness and legislation.

In the fall of 2010, Mary Beth shared her story for the first time with her book, *Choosing to SEE: A Journey of Struggle and Hope* (Revell). This *New York Times* bestselling book was co-authored by Ellen Vaughn, also a *New York Times* bestselling author and an inspirational speaker.

In *Choosing to SEE*, Mary Beth bares her heart and soul as she shares honestly about her personal journey — from her childhood, to challenges of married life, to the sudden and tragic loss of a daughter. *Choosing to SEE* follows her lifelong wrestling match with God, questioning why the life she had planned so carefully doesn't seem to match the plan that God has mapped out for her. The book also explores Mary Beth Chapman's relationship with God in the face of the unexpected, and in the pain of such a brutal loss. Throughout the pages, she tackles these questions with grace, grit, insight and, most of all, hope.

Along with her husband, Mary Beth has also co-authored three books for their Shaoey and Dot children's series, and she continues to write a compelling blog found on her website. She has spoken at numerous Women of Faith conferences, as well as appearing with her family on "A Night with the Chapmans" concert tour last fall.

For more information on Show Hope, visit ShowHope.org, and to keep up with Mary Beth, check out her site at MaryBethChapman. com, where you can also connect with her on Twitter and Facebook.

Thank You

We appreciate all of our wonderful family members and friends, who continue to inspire and teach us on our life's journey. We have been blessed beyond measure with their constant love and support.

We owe huge thanks to all of our contributors. We know that you pour your hearts and souls into the stories that you share with us, and ultimately with each other. We appreciate your willingness to open up your lives to other Chicken Soup for the Soul readers. We can only publish a small percentage of the stories that are submitted, but we read every single one, and even the ones that do not appear in the book have an influence on us and on the final manuscript. We strongly encourage you to continue submitting to future Chicken Soup for the Soul books.

We would like to thank Amy Newmark, our Publisher, for her generous spirit, creative vision, and expert editing. We're also grateful to D'ette Corona, our Assistant Publisher, who seamlessly manages twenty to thirty projects at a time while keeping all of us focused and on schedule. And we'd like to express our gratitude to Barbara LoMonaco, Chicken Soup for the Soul's Webmaster and Editor; and Chicken Soup for the Soul Editor Kristiana Glavin, for her assistance with the final manuscript and proofreading.

We owe a very special thanks to our Creative Director and book producer, Brian Taylor at Pneuma Books, for his brilliant vision for our covers and interiors. And none of this would be possible without the business and creative leadership of our CEO, Bill Rouhana, and our president, Bob Jacobs. Finally, we praise God for guiding us through every step of putting this book together. His presence is truly felt in every page.

Improving Your Life Every Day

Real people sharing real stories—for seventeen years. Now, Chicken Soup for the Soul has gone beyond the bookstore to become a world leader in life improvement. Through books, movies, DVDs, online resources and other partnerships, we bring hope, courage, inspiration and love to hundreds of millions of people around the world. Chicken Soup for the Soul's writers and readers belong to a one-of-a-kind global community, sharing advice, support, guidance, comfort, and knowledge.

Chicken Soup for the Soul stories have been translated into more than forty languages and can be found in more than one hundred countries. Every day, millions of people experience a Chicken Soup for the Soul story in a book, magazine, newspaper or online. As we share our life experiences through these stories, we offer hope, comfort and inspiration to one another. The stories travel from person to person, and from country to country, helping to improve lives everywhere.

Share with Us

We all have had Chicken Soup for the Soul moments in our lives. If you would like to share your story or poem with millions of people around the world, go to chickensoup.com and click on "Submit Your Story." You may be able to help another reader, and become a published author at the same time. Some of our past contributors have launched writing and speaking careers from the publication of their stories in our books!

Our submission volume has been increasing steadily—the quality and quantity of your submissions has been fabulous. We only accept story submissions via our website. They are no longer accepted via mail or fax.

To contact us regarding other matters, please send us an e-mail through webmaster@chickensoupforthesoul.com, or fax or write us at:

Chicken Soup for the Soul
P.O. Box 700
Cos Cob, CT 06807-0700
Fax: 203-861-7194

One more note from your friends at Chicken Soup for the Soul: Occasionally, we receive an unsolicited book manuscript from one of our readers, and we would like to respectfully inform you that we do not accept unsolicited manuscripts and we must discard the ones that appear.

Chicken Soup for the Soul®

Devotional Stories for Women

101 Daily Devotions to Comfort, Encourage, and Inspire Women

Susan M. Heim & Karen Talcott

With a foreword by Jennifer Sands, Christian author and speaker

Throughout time, women have shared their joys and sorrows, thoughts and feelings, experiences and life lessons with one another. The tradition continues in this charming book with 101 stories of friendship, faith, and comfort that affirm God's unconditional love and His wisdom. Women will find encouragement, solace, and strength in these personal stories and prayers that cover everyday trials, tests of faith, marriage, parenting, service to others, and self-esteem.

978-1-935096-48-1

Classics just for Women

Through the ages, mothers have shared their experiences, thoughts, and feelings with one another. The tradition continues in this book in this book of 101 personal stories and prayers by moms about all aspects of motherhood. This book will uplift, counsel, and reassure any woman of faith who needs a boost or reminder of God's ever-present love as she goes through the ups and downs of life and motherhood.

978-1-935096-53-5

Chicken Soup for the Soul

www.chickensoup.com